The Supreme Court
and Constitutional Democracy

The Supreme Court and Constitutional Democracy

John Agresto

Cornell University Press · Ithaca and London

First published 1984 by Cornell University Press.
Second printing 1985.

International Standard Book Number 0-8014-9277-7
Library of Congress Catalog Card Number 83-45928

Printed in the United States of America

*Librarians: Library of Congress cataloging information
appears on the last page of the book.*

*The paper in this book is acid-free and meets the guidelines
for permanence and durability of the Committee on Production
Guidelines for Book Longevity of the Council on Library Resources.*

For my parents,
and the memory of theirs

Contents

The courts ... make no laws, they establish no policy, they never enter the domain of public action. They do not govern.
— JUSTICE DAVID JOSIAH BREWER, 1893

It also was the Supreme Court that made the difficult decision, one that the Congress apparently did not want to make, to lower the voting age to 18. There was nothing in the Constitution that could have suggested that result. In the simplest of terms, the Court decided that when young people were being drafted and asked to go to war and risk their lives at age 18, the time had come to extend to them the right to participate as citizens in the decisions that affected them so seriously.
— JUSTICE LEWIS POWELL, 1979

Preface

Although this is a short book, there is something in it to annoy almost everyone. Conservatives will no doubt find my dismissal of judicial self-restraint and my conditional acceptance of some judicial activism heretical. Liberals should be troubled more, since I attack the rhetorical myths that have been used in the last quarter century to buttress the principle of judicial supremacy and to insulate judicial decisions from any substantial oversight by the Congress or the executive.

This book is an attempt to explore the question "What is the proper role of the Supreme Court in the government of this nation?" Such an inquiry invites us to think historically—to ask about the origins of judicial review in America in the hope of finding compelling arguments or clear insights at its birth. The historical inquiry takes up a good third of the book. But the origins of judicial power are important only insofar as they enlighten us as to the proper scope of the exercise of judicial power: Are there ways to preserve judicial review without inviting judicial supremacy? How can we support the idea of democratic government yet temper it with judicial insight and judicial power? How do we free the Court to be an active contributing agent in the development of our republic yet restrain its potential abuses and correct its inevitable errors? How can we preserve judicial independence yet prevent judicial autocracy? How, in the end, can we use the judiciary to make our laws better, but not to make our laws?

The thesis of the book is simple: contrary to our ordinary and casual view, constitutional interpretation is not and was never intended to be solely within the province of the Court, for constitutional government implies that the ultimate interpreter of our fundamental law is not an autonomous judiciary but the interactive understanding of the people, their representatives, and their judges together. We should see the American political system not as a pyramid, with the Court at the top as the ultimate authority, but rather as an interlocking system of mutual oversight, mutual checking, and combined interpretation.

This view of the Court as a partner in the shaping of constitutional law rather than as its final arbiter has often been recognized as a fact of American political life. We are told—often grudgingly—that the Court is final "only so long as the other branches of government and the political process permit its last word to stand."[1] This book has as part of its aim the justification of that view as theoretically proper, not merely a hard fact of practical politics. The idea of balanced and checked government inherited from the Founders is incompatible with the simple vertical or pyramidal view of constitutional life which most commentators, including the Court, seem to think is the model of American politics.

Nevertheless, despite both philosophical and historical support for the idea that the Court is not the final sovereign of constitutional meaning, practical restraints on judicial autonomy are becoming increasingly difficult to formulate. In part this difficulty is due to the loss of the view that members of Congress themselves have a responsibility to think constitutionally. Increasingly the great debates of Robert Haynes, John C. Calhoun, and Daniel Webster over federalism, or the argument between Alexander Hamilton and Thomas Jefferson over commerce, strike our students as quaint and irrelevant to the process of governing. Today citizens, members of Congress, and presidents alike look to the courts for all constitutional deliberation— that is, for all decisions involving the deepest questions of national direction. At the same time the Court increasingly portrays itself as the final and only authoritative expositor of the constitutional text, augmenting its own authority as its coordinate branches shirk theirs.

The reports of an "imperial judiciary" are hardly idle rumors.[2] Yet the judiciary is imperial not because it is "active," which it is. It is imperial not because it is essentially unchecked, which it also is. It is imperial and exceedingly dangerous because it is active and unchecked in its ability to be the creator, the designer, of new social policy; it has the unhindered ability not simply to prevent legislative acts but to govern affirmatively outside the boundaries of either checks and balances or democratic election. Unlike the older activist Court in this century, the new Court is not antilegislative but itself legislative in the fullest sense: creating categories of expectation and entitlement, ordering the expenditures of great sums of revenue, creating new rights and with them new sanctions. In sum, the courts have assumed "an active role in shaping our society."[3]

The list of contemporary judicial activities at all levels includes running school boards; mandating the construction of new schools and closing old ones; fashioning abortion rights and their attendant privileges, all the way to the hiring and firing of social workers; the governance of mental hospitals and prisons; and the issuance of automotive safety standards.[4] Rather than acting as a check on precipitous social change—the "sober second thought" of an older constitutional understanding[5]—the courts are now themselves the agents of social change, with no candidates for the role of sober second thinkers in sight. We know how to check our legislatures; we do not know how to check our legislative judiciary. Nor can we forget that rights enunciated and policy initiated by judges begin quickly to have a life of their own. Congress will therefore find the activism of today's courts, which initiate policies and pronounce new views of constitutional entitlements and rights, much harder to control than the nay-saying activism of any previous courts. For all these reasons, the tempering of the judicial power becomes all the more imperative as it also becomes all the more difficult.

This shift in the nature of judicial activism from negative to affirmative activity has been not only a political but a jurisprudential phenomenon.* The cautionary writings of an older line of academic legal writers, from James B. Thayer to Edward S. Corwin to Alexander Bickel, have effectively been replaced by theoretical efforts that are systematically directed at the expansion of judicial power and the mitigation of any effective internal or external restraints on judicial activity.

In this regard at least two recent books deserve mention. John Hart Ely's *Democracy and Distrust* is perhaps the most ingenious of all recent attempts to support a particular theory of judicial power. Cognizant of the pitfalls, Ely rejects the notion that the Court should be in the business of fashioning substantive principles out of the commodious language of the Constitution. Rather, Ely would limit the Court to "ensuring broad participation in the processes and distributions of government"—policing both equal access to political decision making and overseeing the "bounty" and the "benefits" that citizens

---

*In politics, the shift of the judiciary from negative activist to affirmative activist partly explains the change in both conservative and liberal attitudes toward the Court. So long as the Court was one more roadblock in the way of precipitous economic or social change, conservatives tended to praise it as a bulwark of constitutional government. As the Court became more and more the independent agent of such changes, most American liberals easily accommodated themselves to the new judicial activism. Only those liberals who, while agreeing with many of the Court's decisions, still recognize the undemocratic nature of judicial activism and fear a judicial change of heart are torn by these developments.

receive from government.[6] Yet, like *Marbury* v. *Madison*, in which John Marshall augmented the Court's overall authority by denying it power over one particular, Ely's construct would work to solidify judicial activism on a seemingly narrow but actually quite pervasive theory of equal access and equal result, a theory that finds scarcely any warrant in the Constitution itself.* Indeed, as Ely notes, the most systematic process-policing Court, the Warren Court, was by that fact alone able to be the most active in decreeing substantive results couched in the terms of process.[7] Such an approach is clearly of no help in any attempt to restrain the autonomy of today's judges.

Jesse Choper's *Judicial Review and the National Political Process* is more forthrightly on the side of judicial expansionism. Like Ely, Choper argues that the Court must exercise its powers to protect those rights "not adequately represented in the political process." Why? Because "custodianship . . . should be assigned to a governing body that is insulated from political responsibility"(!) and because "almost by definition the processes of democracy bode ill for the security of personal rights." As I hope to show in this book, not only are these sentiments generally false, they are, taken together, nothing more than an undisguised brief for judicial oligarchy. And to state categorically that "the Supreme Court is the most effective guarantor of the interests of the unpopular and unrepresented precisely because it is the most politically isolated judicial body" is to have a rather

---

*"When it came to describing the actual mechanics of republican government in the Constitution, however, this concern for equality got comparatively little explicit attention" (John Hart Ely, *Democracy and Distrust* [Cambridge: Harvard University Press, 1980], p. 79). Ely tries to excuse this oversight by arguing that the Founders were careless because they mistakenly thought "that the people were an essentially homogeneous group whose interests did not vary significantly." Yet this is so obviously not the case that Ely quickly begins to abandon the argument (pp. 80–81), and we are left to wonder how, despite the Founders, this particular vision of equality has now become the key to constitutional meaning.

playful attitude not only toward all the standard canons of logic but also toward the historical record itself.[8]*

The contemporary debate over judicial power revolves around a number of our most potent ideas—liberty, equality, democracy, and representation. These were formative principles when we first wrote our Constitution and established our Court. Moreover, these have been the principles through which we have tried to understand our Constitution, judge the role of the Court, and evaluate the use of its powers. It is now through these principles—liberty, equality, democracy, and representation—that we can and must assess the Court. Yet we must remember that the reverse is also true: Henceforth our view of the Court and its powers will direct, for better or worse, the future life of equality, liberty, and democratic government itself.

This book began as a paper written for a seminar on constitutionalism led by Paul Sigmund and later delivered on a panel of the American Political Science Association chaired by Wilson Carey McWilliams. Thanks to their help, and the help of many others, it expanded, slowly, into this book. Among the others who bear some responsibility for not having stopped it before it grew are William Bennett, Terry Eastland, Edward Erler, Walter Berns, Christopher Wolfe, Sanford Lakoff, and William Leuchtenburg. I am also grateful to the *Georgia Law Review* for publishing portions of Chapters 4 and 5 and for

---

*These views regarding the moral sanctity of the Court and the illiberal nature of majority rule or congressional authority—notions barely defensible and rarely enunciated before the moral triumph of the *Brown* decision—are quickly becoming today's new orthodoxy. "As a matter of comparative institutional competence," Michael Perry has recently written, "the politically insulated federal judiciary is more likely, when the human rights issue is a deeply controversial one, to move us in the direction of a right answer" (Michael J. Perry, *The Constitution, the Courts, and Human Rights* [New Haven: Yale University Press, 1983], p. 102). Richard Neely and Ronald Dworkin have argued in much the same vein and (I hope to show) equally unpersuasively. See Richard Neely, *How Courts Govern America* (New Haven: Yale University Press, 1981), and Ronald Dworkin, *Taking Rights Seriously* (Cambridge: Harvard University Press, 1977).

permission to use them here. Thanks are due above all to the administration, support staff, and fellows of the National Humanities Center in North Carolina. This book cannot begin to repay them for their generosity, their helpfulness, and their care. Their generosity was equaled only by the patience of Catherine, my wife, who heard me say "It's just about done" for years, and smiled.

JOHN AGRESTO

Washington, D.C.

The Supreme Court
and Constitutional Democracy

1 *The Limits of Judicial Power*

> In the arguments in favor of a declaration of rights,
> you omit one which has great weight with me, the legal
> check which it puts into the hands of the judiciary. This
> is a body, which if rendered independent, and kept
> strictly to their own department, merits great confi-
> dence for their learning and integrity.
>
> —THOMAS JEFFERSON

> We have seen, too, that contrary to all correct example,
> they are in the habit of going out of the question before
> them, to throw an anchor ahead, and grapple further
> hold for future advances of power. They are then in
> fact, the corps of sappers and miners....
>
> —THOMAS JEFFERSON

A peculiar mystery surrounds the Supreme Court. I mean here not the secrecy of its deliberations or the awesome nature of its trappings—its robes, its grand temple, or any of the vestiges of antique veneration still connected to American magistracy and law. The curious, the mysterious fact about the United States Supreme Court is that its function, its appropriate role— its very justification—is often indistinct or confused in our minds.

Not that we fail to understand what the Court does; we know, for instance, that it helps to govern and direct the polity through the interpretation and application of the law, including the law of the Constitution. Our difficulty stems not from confusion over what the Court does but from conflicting notions, or no notions at all, as to why it does it. We should begin, then, by putting the question bluntly: Why is it that the Court has judicial review?

The first and often predominant answer to that question is the legal-historical response: the Founders intended the Court to have this power. American constitutional scholarship has always concerned itself with the debate over the intentions of the Founders and the true origins of judicial power. The concern is surely a valid one, for within the Founders' intentions are viewpoints that must be seen and arguments that must be understood. And intent, when discovered, binds us in law. But, as we all know, America has thought it fitting, again through law, to modify or abandon the Founders' intent on any number of serious issues, from the reeligibility of the president and the election of senators to the status of slavery and the requirements for citizenship. As a philosophic argument the intent of the Founders need not be compelling—it can carry weight only insofar as the intent is reasonable and persuasive. If the Founders intended judicial review, we should know why; if not, why not. They would have wanted it no other way.

Thus, although the power of judicial review may be traceable to the framers' original intent, it will gain its justification only from deliberative argument. At this point in our search for reasons for the Court's power we are often confronted not by silence but by an impressive chorus of strong voices. Yet the voices often sing not only different but discordant lines.

Judicial Power and Constitutional Government

On one side there is the venerable argument that looks on the Court as the Founders' protective barrier against unconstitutional acts, our security against political usurpation. The justices, in this account, stand as *defensores fidei*, as the watchmen in the constitutional edifice. The argument is venerable because it has its roots in the first ages of judicial review. No less a figure than Alexander Hamilton observed that "the courts of justice are to be considered as the bulwarks of a limited constitution," as an "excellent barrier to . . . encroachments and oppressions."[1] Like Peter at the gates, the Court, in this account, holds the keys to the Constitution, letting through those laws and acts that pass the test, rejecting those found wanting.

There are, of course, more and less subtle varieties of this understanding. In its coarser forms come visions of varying degrees of "mechanical jurisprudence"—the putting of the questionable law next to the Constitution to see if it "squares." The best-known judicial statement of this position is Justice Owen Roberts': "When an act of Congress is appropriately challenged in the courts as not conforming to the constitutional mandate the judicial branch of the government has only one duty,—to lay the article of the Constitution which is invoked beside the statute which is challenged and to decide whether the latter squares with the former."[2]* On that level judges become the defenders of the Constitution because they are honest officials of goodwill who can read well. At this extreme it is their judicial dispassion that makes us rest easy in their guardianship.

John Marshall began, more convincingly, from a contrary perspective: it was in fact the very passion of the judicial branch, its passion for the rule of law, that made the Court the proper guardian of the Constitution. "It is emphatically the province and duty of the judicial department to say what the law is." Moreover—as the partisans of this position affirm—although all

---

*One is tempted, after the fact, to suggest that there be a moratorium on the use of this statement as the perennial whipping boy in works on the judiciary. Such a moratorium is unlikely, however, because the statement expresses with all the grandeur of precise simplicity a variant of an old and still widely held—or wished for—view of the judicial function.

officers of the government swear an oath to uphold the Constitution, the oath "certainly applies in an especial manner to [judges'] conduct in their official capacity."[3] Other political officials, since they are not jurists, may often overstep their constitutional bounds simply in the pursuit of what seem to them to be wholesome and desirable public policies. "The members of the legislature," Hamilton argues, "will rarely be chosen with a view to those qualifications which fit men for the stations of judges."[4] But those whose oath applies in an "especial" manner because they are jurists, professionals of the law rather than of policy, are appropriately thoughtful guardians of our constitutional will. When this perspective is coupled with the fact that justices are carefully selected by the executive and confirmed by the Senate, then given safe tenure and secure salaries, the task of justifying judicial review seems at an end. Our Court (this position affirms) is select, expert, and independent, bound only by our will as we have expressed it constitutionally. On this basis alone Hamilton seems justified in referring to the justices as "faithful guardians of the Constitution."[5]

Still, as by now we know, this carefully drawn argument is hardly a persuasive justification. It raises, to give only one obvious objection, a difficult question of fact: Is the Court, or has it been, this proper guardian of our Constitution? Objections on this score could be multiplied with ease, even by a researcher whose only material included what Courts have remarked about the fidelity of their predecessors to the constitutional text. Opinions, of course, will differ. But there precisely is the crux of the issue. The judgments of the Court—the "opinions" of the justices, as the word is properly used even by them—necessarily bear the marks of individual assessment, of individual perspectives, insights, understandings, and even individually formulated goals. This admixture of judicial insight is, to be sure, involved in the very essence of proper constitutional development—the organic law partly gains its life from the vitality of judicial insight. But it is always at first *their* insight, *their* judgment. And even if the separation of judgment from will were as clear as Hamilton described it,* we would still need the assurance that cannot always be given—that the judgment of justices is the judgment of the Constitution.†

Finally, if we put aside questions of fact as to the faithful

---

*The discussion of will and judgment is in *The Federalist*, ed. Jacob E. Cooke (Middletown, Conn: Wesleyan University Press, 1961), no. 78, p. 523. Marshall, in an analysis that most scholars find unconvincing, made much the same point about judicial will in Osborn v. Bank of the United States, 9 Wheaton 738 (1824), 866:

> Judicial power, as contradistinguished from the power of the laws, has no existence. Courts are mere instruments of the law, and can will nothing. When they are said to exercise a discretion, it is a mere legal discretion, a discretion to be exercised in discerning the course prescribed by law; and, when that is discerned, it is the duty of the court to follow it. Judicial power is never exercised for the purpose of giving effect to the will of the judge; always for the purpose of giving effect to the will of the legislature; or, in other words, to the will of the law.

†We can here lay aside two strident objections to judicial "objectivity," although not without recognizing the elements of actual truth contained in them. First, there is a body of behavioral literature on the Court which argues in part that judicial "judgments" are reducible to private "attitudes," attitudes shaped by former experiences, personal predispositions, and so on. Students of the Court are probably most familiar with the work of Glendon Schubert in this area. See, for example, his *Judicial Behavior* (Chicago: Rand McNally, 1964). But reference should also be made to previous works in "legal realism"—Jerome Frank, *Law and the Modern Mind* (New York: Coward, 1930); Karl N. Llewellyn, *The Bramble Bush: On Law and Its Study* (New York: Oceana, 1930); and Llewellyn, "The Constitution as an Institution," *Columbia Law Review* 34 (1934): 1–40. Perhaps insofar as no judicial opinion exists uninformed by some already held understanding, some "attitude" as to what is licit or proper or necessary, the position speaks an obvious truth. John Adams knew as much when he stayed up late at night making Federalist, not Jeffersonian-Republican, appointments.

The second objection to the easy equation of judicial judgment and constitutional command is Jefferson's. In his view the danger went beyond reading the law in terms of predispositions, attitudes, and private values: rather it promised to be worse—the use of the judicial position to augment the judges' own power and personal influence. "Our judges are," he wrote, "as honest as other men, and not more so. They have, with others, the same passion for party, for power and for the privilege of their corps" (Jefferson to William Charles Jarvis, September 28, 1820, in *The Writings of Thomas Jefferson*, ed. Andrew A. Lipscomb, 20 vols. [Washington, D.C.: Thomas Jefferson Memorial Association, 1905], 15:277; see also pp. 297–98 and 486–87). Often, it seems, the love of power is even stronger in judges than in other people; see ibid., 1:120–22 ("they . . . throw an anchor ahead, and grapple further hold for

guardianship of the Court over the constitutional text, other questions still emerge: Is the Court the only defender? Is it the last defender? And in what areas, if any, can we rest most confidently in its judgments?

Judicial Review and the Protection of Individual Rights

When we consider whether there are any areas in which the constitutional judgment of the Court is especially trustworthy, the evidence seems at first to be particularly clear. Regarding "adherence to the rights ... of individuals," the Court would necessarily be "inflexible and uniform." "The general liberty of the people," Hamilton remarked, "can never be endangered from that quarter."[6] Here begins the most prevalent of the modern defenses of the judicial power; here today's defenders of judicial review have marshaled their arguments and collected their evidence: the Court is especially necessary to protect from subversion or erosion the constitutional rights of all individuals.[7]

Although Jefferson would later oppose expansive judicial power, he originally connected judicial review to the preservation of civil liberties. As we noted at the start of this chapter, Jefferson wrote Madison that a declaration of rights would help buttress the judiciary's legal check on legislative power. If judicial powers were both independent and well defined, the judges' "learning and integrity" would effectively prevent the erosion of public liberty.[8] Madison, never one to forget a valuable argument, repeated and developed much the same sentiment in the congressional debate over the ratification of the Bill of Rights. Against the objection that a declaration of right would be an ineffectual "paper barrier" to illiberal usurpation, Madison re-

---

future advances of power"). The only time Jefferson had what might be called a Federalist understanding of the irremedial defects of human nature was when he reflected on Federalists and on judges.

plied with the best general view of the libertarian function of an active court: "If they [that is, statements of reserved rights] are incorporated into the Constitution, independent tribunals of justice will consider themselves in a peculiar manner the guardians of those rights; they will be an impenetrable bulwark against every assumption of power in the Legislative or Executive; they will be naturally led to resist every encroachment upon rights expressly stipulated for in the Constitution by the declaration of rights."[9]

It is exactly this notion of the Court as the ultimate and effective partisan of constitutional and individual rights that Chief Justice Marshall seized upon in defense of judicial power in *Marbury* v. *Madison.* The only examples Marshall gives of judicial review in action are hypothetical instances of legislative attacks on fundamental liberties: illegal taxation, bills of attainder, *ex post facto* laws, and attempts to weaken a citizen's security against being declared a traitor.[10] So, when Eugene Rostow wrote that "the Court sits as the ultimate guardian of the liberties on which the democratic effectiveness of political action depends," he not only summarized the ground on which the most prevalent modern defense of judicial review rests but repeated a view seemingly hallowed in its American antiquity.[11] A select and independent Court—free from the legislator's necessary attachment to various economic, religious, and narrow political interests—has every incentive to be a partisan not only of the constitutional text itself but especially of "the general liberty of the people."[12]

Although current statements describing the Court as the champion of individual liberties could be easily collected and multiplied, the remarkable fact is that in the formative period of judicial review, such arguments were uncommon, even rare. The major statements have already been alluded to, including parts of Marshall's formulation in *Marbury.* Yet it is hardly the case that the Founders were unconcerned about the necessary requirements for establishing a liberal nation. While critics may take issue with their understanding of liberty within their vision of the just society, or dispute their means of achieving it, the fact remains that the writers and supporters of the Constitution discussed the idea of liberty with a thoroughness and a devotion that verged on singlemindedness. Daily the Federal Convention debated, for example, whether liberty was more secure under greater or lesser centralization, with more or less democratic power, through simple or more complex mechanisms, in small countries or in large republics. These concerns were repeated and developed in *The Federalist,* in the debates in the state ratifying conventions, in the public press, and in the precedent-setting first Congresses. Still, the topic of judicial review arose only sporadically.

Reasons for this situation are hardly obscure. Simply put, the Court was not widely regarded as our foremost guardian of liberty. Such a faith would have seemed to the Founders to be overly simplistic and potentially quite dangerous. It was rather the totality of the interactive constitutional mechanisms that would finally be the surest protection of human liberties in a just society, and not any single organ of that government. As Madison pointed out, the primary protection against political oppression destructive of individual rights and interests would initially be set in the diversity and scope of the nation itself: "In the extended republic of the United States, and among the great variety of interests, parties and sects which it embraces, a coalition of a majority of the whole society could seldom take place on any other principles than those of justice and the general good."[13] To this major social defense against despotic government the Founders added other, more political precautions. There, listed among these varied political checks on precipitous as well as tyrannic power, was included the power of judicial review. These "auxiliary precautions" (as *The Federalist* labels them) encompassed bicameralism, diverse modes and times of election, separation of powers with a modified check in each branch, and, at base, the direct or indirect connection of all branches to the will of the electorate.[14] "It is remarkable," Thayer wrote almost a century ago, "how small a part [the idea of the

Court as a major defender of liberty] played in any of the debates. The chief protections were a wide suffrage, short terms of office, a double legislative chamber and the so-called executive veto."[15]

Intriguing as the early discussion of judicial power and liberal government may be, even more remarkable is the fact that there is no consistent correlation whatever between the growth of judicial authority and increases in social justice or in the protection of personal liberty. The truth is that throughout the history of America the Court has hardly been the great or consistent champion of individual rights. Far more often the exercise of judicial review, especially as against national legislation, has been oppressive to the cause of human rights rather than restrictive of illiberal legislation. To understand why the Court may not be the nation's foremost guardian of individual rights, we should first review some history and then return to the level of theory.

For every case destructive of racial segregation or liberating to the press and supportive of the free flow of information or helpful to those who labor under poverty, ignorance, unfair accusation, or the shadow of social malice, other cases can be cited with greater force to support the view of judicial power as fundamentally unfriendly to human or civil rights, unnecessarily illiberal in its judgment, and oppressive in its result. The sorriest fact is that such a list would be heavily weighted not with cases in which the Court deferred to the illiberality of the more political branches but with cases in which the Court, invoking the name of either the Constitution or of liberty, itself voided liberating and progressive as well as necessary legislation. Some of these cases are rightly famous: *Dred Scott* v. *Sandford* denied federal authority to regulate or prohibit the extension of slavery into United States territory; *United States* v. *Reese* invalidated a federal statute that had forbidden state election officials to deny to any person entitled to do so the right to cast a vote; *United States* v. *Cruikshank* decided that the rights of assembly, life, liberty, and the franchise were not federal rights and therefore could not be protected by Congress (for the security of these rights the freed slaves needed to depend on state protection); *United States* v. *Harris* voided the 1871 Anti-Lynching Act that made conspiracy to deprive a person of the equal protection of the law a federal crime; *The Civil Rights Cases* overturned the Civil Rights Act of 1875 that had outlawed segregation and racial discrimination in public accommodations, conveyances, and places of public amusement; *Adair* v. *United States* held a federal attempt to prevent interstate employers from firing union laborers to be a violation of the Fifth Amendment; *Hammer* v. *Dagenhart* voided the first child-labor law; *Bailey* v. *Drexel Furniture Company* voided the Child Labor Tax Act of 1919; *Adkins* v. *Children's Hospital* held that a minimum wage for women workers in the District of Columbia was in violation of the Fifth Amendment.[16] This list includes only some reversals of federal statutes, and it ends without enumerating the many early New Deal cases in which the Court did damage to both itself and the nation, and from which it ultimately beat an embarrassed retreat. There are many others—*Baldwin* v. *Franks*, *James* v. *Bowman*, *Hodges* v. *United States*, *Butts* v. *Merchant and Mines Transportation Company*, *Nichols* v. *Coolidge*, *Untermyer* v. *Anderson*, *Heiner* v. *Donnan* (to name only a very few)—which are now charitably obscure.*

*Baldwin v. Franks, 120 U.S. 678 (1887), held that federal protection against conspiracy, denied in the Harris case as it applied to citizens, would also be denied as it applied to aliens. James v. Bowman, 190 U.S. 127 (1903), voided federal law penalizing "every person who prevents, hinders, controls, or intimidates another from exercising the right of suffrage ... guaranteed by the Fifteenth Amendment ... by means of bribery or threats." Hodges v. United States, 203 U.S. 1 (1906), voided the provision of the Civil Rights Act of 1870 that gave to "all persons within the jurisdiction of the United States" the same right "to make and enforce contracts ... as is enjoyed by white citizens." Butts v. Merchant and Mines Transportation Co., 230 U.S. 126 (1913), denied the power of the Civil Rights Act of 1875 to protect the rights of Negroes with regard to travel and accommodation on the high seas or in the District of Columbia, thus finally eliminating the application or enforcement of that act anywhere. Nichols v. Coolidge, 274 U.S. 531 (1927); Untermyer v. Anderson, 276 U.S. 440 (1928); and Heiner v. Donnan, 285 U.S., 312 (1932), restrained the federal government from taxing the estates or gifts of the wealthy.

If we wish to narrow our investigation, we may profitably look at the Court's reaction to congressional attempts to restrict the use of child labor. The first legislation on the subject, passed in 1916, was voided by the Court in 1918.[17] The Congress soon tried again, this time acting under its taxing powers rather than under the commerce clause; but again, in 1922, the Court struck the legislation down.[18] The Congress acted once more in 1938, and finally, in 1941, the Court relented.[19] That the Court did, in the end, give in, after three congressional attempts in twenty-five years, is hardly supportive of the argument that the judiciary is a fortress of social concern central to the protection of liberty against power. Nor is the fact of the Court's final surrender to the more progressive forces of the democracy any consolation for the quarter of a century of "ruined lives" (as Holmes put it) for which its misconstructions bear some sure responsibility.* And the situation is, of course, worse, in both scope and devastation, when one enters the field of race relations in the century following *Dred Scott*. As Leonard Levy once wrote, the idea that the Court has been valuable in securing the blessings of liberty cannot "command the preponderance of historical evidence."

> For example, one may say ... that it is true as a matter of experience that a vigorous lead from the Supreme Court inhibits or weakens popular responsibility in the areas of liberty, equality and justice. The subject of Negro rights is indeed the best of illustrations. Bearing in mind that the Court is an institution of enormous prestige whose declaration of principles teaches and leads the nation in the making of public policy, one cannot doubt the pernicious, highly undemocratic influence of the series of decisions in which the Court crippled and voided most of the comprehensive program for protecting the civil rights of Negroes after the Civil War. These decisions paralyzed or supplanted legislative and community action, created bigotry, and played a crucial role in destroying public opinion that fa-

---

*The full sentence is in Holmes's dissent in Hammer: "It is not for this Court to pronounce when prohibition is necessary to regulation if it ever may be necessary—to say that it is permissible as against strong drink but not as against the product of ruined lives" (247 U.S., 251 [1918], 280).

vored meeting the challenge of the Negro problem as a constitutional—that is, a moral—obligation.[20]

"If the test of the value of judicial review to the preservation of basic liberties were to be rested on consideration of actual invalidations," as John G. Frank once wrote, "the balance would be against judicial review."[21] Or, as Levy himself wrote in summarizing part of the evidence: "Over the course of our history, in other words, judicial review has worked out badly."[22]

This is, obviously, not the whole picture. If it were, no democratic nation with any dedication to human rights would have tolerated the Court this long. But that history speaks more truth than we have a right to be comfortable with.

If we return to the level of theory previously under investigation, two things will now become clearer. First, the Founders' prediction has been generally fulfilled: an extensive republic encompassing such a great plurality of sects, opinions, and desires, all channeled into a government of limited powers, divided and then checked in the very process of legislating, has rarely been legislatively oppressive or illiberal. Again to recur to Madisonian theory, if we extend the sphere of the Republic so as to embrace, at the national level, that great plurality of opinions, sects, and factional desires, if we "take in a greater variety of parties and interests," we immediately "make it less probable that a majority of the whole will have a common motive to invade the rights of other citizens." And if, within the very structure of the government, we further divide and fracture that popular will institutionally for the purpose of enacting legislation, it becomes even more certain that "a coalition of the whole could seldom take place on any other principles than those of justice and the general good."[23] The will of a national majority enacted into law will generally contain ample protection for the security of minority rights well before such legislation reaches the courts.

But we can make a second observation that goes even further: merely on the basis of statistical probability, an institution that voided legislation that had survived the rigors of the internal legislative scheme that the Founders developed would rarely be voiding "tyrannical" legislation. All too often what the Court would nullify would be the concerted opinion of the democracy filtered through various chambers and modes of election and refined by time and compromise. Such legislation may well be so compromised as to fall short of being *effective*, but it will only rarely be oppressive or despotic. The odds are, in other words, against an easy equation of an active Court with liberty or social justice. At the level of national legislation, a Court whose primary mission is to check legislation will only on the rarest occasions be checking illiberal or oppressive enactments. It is more likely to find itself hindering compromised, benign, fair, and often long-overdue legislation.

Nor is this situation changed merely by the Court's declaration that henceforward it will pay particular heed to matters involving alleged violation of right or by declaring itself to be especially liberal. No magic transforms a court from illiberal to liberal because it declares as its mission the protection of rights; the pre-1937 Court honestly and neatly categorized many of its idiosyncratic economic views under the idea of "*liberty* of contract." It, too, thought itself faithful to the dictates of the Bill of Rights and the Fourteenth Amendment. Nor can a court become enlightened merely by deciding to turn away from economic concerns and focus its attention on the freedom of individuals. There is no simple alchemy that transforms judicial activism into an unalloyed defense of right.

In the end, any argument for judicial review which points to the idea that the Court has been America's greatest protector of individual rights will find itself on less than secure ground. The modern defense of judicial power which sees the Court as, by its nature, a liberal institution and the protector of minorities from oppressive majorities requires of us too much historical and philosophical forgetting.

Judicial Review and Democratic Government

So far, our consideration of America's dedication to the Constitution and to the principles of liberty and equality seems not to have given us any solid justification for the practice of judicial review, at least not at the level of national politics. But, beyond dedication to equal liberty and constitutional rule, America is also devoted to a particular form of government: democracy. Knowing, with Lincoln, that "unanimity is impossible; the rule of a minority, as a permanent arrangement, is wholly inadmissible,"[24] we put our future in the hands of a restrained democracy—restrained, to be sure (for that is the whole idea behind constitutionalism), but democratic in the end nonetheless.* But here, we are sometimes told, may well be the best argument *for* judicial review. "All too will bear in mind this sacred principle," Jefferson taught us, "that though the will of the majority is in all cases to prevail, that will, to be rightful, must be reasonable."[25] If the Court can exercise its power of review to help perfect democratic life—to make its will "reasonable" and to give public opinion greater insight, substance, breadth, and constitutional wisdom—then our search for the best defense of judicial review will have come to a satisfactory completion.

The partisans of this defense of judicial review begin their analysis with a lesson in democracy. "It is an error to insist that no society is democratic unless it has a government of unlimited powers."[26] On the basis of that truth the defenders of judicial review have further observed that the courts are generally no more than temporary brakes on the popular will—exactly that salutary restraint which allows time for democratic sober second thoughts. Thus the exercise of judicial review, Benjamin Cardozo remarked, "tends to stabilize and rationalize the legislative judgment, to infuse it with the glow of principle."[27]

This position is inviting; it certainly seems to be in line with the Founders' grand design of mitigating the defects of dem-

---

*Not that we revere only absolute majoritarianism. We usually recognize, with the Founders, that a pure democracy is less desirable than a modified representative democracy. Nevertheless, we also recognize, after all is said and done, that the "fundamental maxim of republican government ... requires that the sense of the majority should prevail" and not the will of any segment of the whole society (*Federalist*, no. 22, p. 139).

ocratic government without jettisoning democratic rule itself. But this analysis, too, has trouble with history. The checking activity of the Court—its ability to give us second thoughts about ourselves—seems hardly sobering, given the objects to which that power has historically attached itself: the voiding of personal liberty laws, of national power to restrict slavery in the territories, of a federal income tax, of national economic regulation under the taxing and commerce power, and so on. The sobering nature of a judicial check on national legislation is a notion more elegant in theory than in actual practice.

Recognizing the problematic nature of any defense of judicial power that rests on the way the checking power of the Court has refined, moderated, or broadened democratic opinion, other defenders of the role of the judiciary within a democracy point not to the Court's efficacy but to its powerlessness. "The fact is," as Robert Dahl once wrote in one of the most widely quoted articles in the field of constitutional law, "that the policy views dominant on the Court are never long out of line with the policy views dominant among the lawmaking majorities of the United States. Consequently it would be most unrealistic to suppose that the Court would, for more than a few years at most, stand against any major alternatives sought by a lawmaking majority."[28] "It is difficult," another student of the Court once wrote, "to find a major decision denying Congress authority to do something which it does not do today."[29] But if the Court always does fall in line with the popular will after holding up legislation for a time (twenty-five years, for example, in the case of all child labor laws), the power of judicial review hardly seems worth the bother. If the argument contained in such scholarship is to be believed, the Court's function seems to be to take national legislation (which is itself often too little too late), prevent its effectuation for some time, and then relent.*

---

*A widely held variation of the view that the Court ultimately falls in line or follows the election returns is the notion that writers of textbooks often seem to prefer—that the opinions of the Court are democratic because they really "mirror" or "reflect" the true spirit of their age. Thus, when the Court vitiated the great Civil Rights acts of the Reconstruction period, it was reflecting

One of the more lasting consequences of the judicial revolution initiated by the Warren Court is that such an analysis no longer seems even barely plausible. The contemporary objections to judicial activity are not that courts have been checking legislation but that they have been legislating in their own name. Judges do not ask us to reconsider our social policies: the democracy has been put in the position of having to ask judges to reconsider theirs. Though the current attack on "judicial imperialism" has much the same vocabulary as, for example, the enemies of the old laissez-faire Court of the Depression, the judicial activity itself is markedly different. Today the courts are seen as autocratic and imperial for making and carrying out social policy beyond the general popular will expressed politically, *not* primarily because they have checked legislation. The current furor over judicial activism has arisen because the Court obviously has more than a delaying effect on policy and legislation. In fact, ever since the tenure of Chief Justice Earl Warren, no one could doubt that the Court shapes policy and more often leads than follows public opinion. The decisions on reapportionment, desegregation, obscenity, and abortion are all appropriate to mention here. A checking court might well always lose to the forces of democracy in time; but a court that takes it upon itself to advance the vistas of right and power is not fighting those rear-guard losing battles of years past.

---

general American racial feelings; when it chipped away at federal attempts to regulate the monopolies or aid labor unions or restrict child labor or set minimum wages, it mirrored the laissez-faire sentiments of all Americans. But such an analysis would have to explain how, if the true American spirit was really against such legislative acts, the statutes came to exist in the first place; how, that is, laws that favored the working classes became law not only against the retardant effects of the whole constitutional system (separate houses, presidential veto) but against strong regional and highly vocal economic interests. That the Court, at various times, lags behind the popular will (as in the 1930s), or acts against it, or in fact helps to shape it (as in the present era, beginning in the 1950s) seem all more tenable than the view that the Court in exercising judicial review acts as the true expression of the popular feeling against the other political branches.

Here exactly is where the power of the judiciary runs afoul of democratic theory. It simply cannot be said that, by itself, "the Court is almost powerless to affect the course of national policy."[30] As one modern judicial critic has written:

> The courts have truly changed their role in American life. American courts, the most powerful in the world . . . are now far more powerful than ever before; public opinion—which Tocqueville, Bryce, and other analysts thought would control the courts as well as so much else in American life—is weaker. . . . And the courts, through interpretation of the Constitution and the laws, now reach into the lives of the people, against the will of the people, deeper than they ever have in American history.[31]

No one who examines the Court's recent directives over schooling, political rights, the death penalty, race relations, "affirmative action," the rights of the accused, and the rights covered by the rubric of "privacy" can deny the general validity of this observation. Like "the Justiciary of Aragon," to which John Dickinson referred in the convention of 1787, the American judiciary has become "by degrees the law giver."[32] The test that Charles Black mentions in *The People and the Court*, of paging through the United States Code to remind ourselves how little of it could be initiated by the courts, seems no longer very persuasive.* Now neither the sword nor the purse is completely beyond judicial hands. And Hamilton's notion that judges "can take no

*The full passage is:

> Flip through any volume of the United States Statute at large and ask yourself which of the actions of Congress there recorded could have been taken by the Court, under the widest theories that have ever prevailed, or even been put forward, on the subject of judicial review. To speak of such an institution as 'supreme' in the sphere of policy-making is ridiculous. The very most the Court ever has is a veto.   [Charles L. Black, *The People and the Court* (Englewood Cliffs, N.J.: Prentice-Hall, 1960), p. 168]

The reader should compare this statement with the long catalogue of policy activity—from welfare administration to employment policy to busing and racial quotas to prison reform to abortion rules—initiated and carried out by the contemporary judiciary described in Nathan Glazer, "Towards an Imperial Judiciary?" *Public Interest*, Fall 1975, pp. 104–23, or in Donald L. Horowitz, *The Courts and Social Policy* (Washington, D.C.: Brookings Institution, 1978).

active resolution whatever" hardly describes the current situation.[33]

In this context, it is insufficient to argue that rule by the Court is nonetheless "democratic" because we have "accepted" its directive influence. True, judicial review is "a people's institution, confirmed by the people through history."[34] But the real tension between democratic rule and judicial power cannot be swept away with such formulations; the role of the Court is hardly made democratic because the people have submitted to it. On that scale even hereditary monarchy, once accepted by the people, could be called democracy.* Democracy means that the people have full power to control their destinies, not that they have tacitly (or, worse, grudgingly) consented to the directive rule of others.†

All attempts to blur the tension between judicial review and democratic government ultimately fail. The fact is that the Court is in essence only marginally connected to democratic choice. Its justices—unelected, life tenured in practice, with secure salaries—have plenary power over the interpretation of the nation's fundamental law and authority to direct private and public activity in accord with their opinion of the demands of that Constitution. And when the Court uses that authority to stand against the democratic will or to direct public policy, we are unsure what to think, much less what to do about it.

Uneasy with the notion of an institution essentially removed from the democratic process but with final interpretive powers

---

*Consider Robert Dahl: "No amount of tampering with democratic theory can conceal the fact that a system in which the policy preferences of minorities prevail over majorities is at odds with the traditional criteria for distinguishing a democracy from other political systems" ("Decision Making in a Democracy: The Supreme Court as National Policy Maker," *Journal of Public Law* 6 [1958]:283. "Whenever the Court strikes down legislation," as Judge J. Skelly Wright remarked, "it says to the majority that it may not have its own way" ("The Role of the Supreme Court in a Democratic Society," *Cornell Law Review* 54 [November 1968]:12).

†"The cool and deliberate sense of the community ought in all governments and actually will in all free governments utlimately prevail over the views of its rulers" (*Federalist*, no. 63 [Madison], p. 425).

over the people's organic law, many serious commentators have called for prudential restrictions—primarily self-restrictions—on the exercise of judicial power.[35] Like earlier scholars who tried to confine judicial review by questioning or denying the Founders' intent to establish such a power, modern advocates of judicial restraint begin with the insight that the Court is (in Felix Frankfurter's words) "inherently oligarchic"—"the non-democratic organ of our government."[36]

But the demand for judicial self-restraint is hardly a sufficient solution to the problem of judicial power within a democracy. The demand for self-restraint is usually ineffectual when addressed to most holders of political power. It may be especially fruitless when those holders of power can also see themselves as possessing special insight into constitutional mandates and constitutional right. In addition, the partisans of judicial self-restraint, who are generally perceptive students of the constitutional foundations of American political institutions, should find the idea of *self*-restraint an anomaly in a system purposefully built on layers of *external* restraints. The genius that animated all of our politics was that each and every institution (not to mention every faction and individual) could be freed—allowed to be *active*—because each would be balanced and checked. To be active without a check is tyranny; but a self-generated check on activity may well undermine the possibility of great contributions.*

*Perhaps the most eloquent judicial defense of self-restraint is Frankfurter's dissent in West Virginia Board of Education v. Barnette, 319 U.S. 624 (1943), 646–71. But that very case, more than any other, shows how the principle of restraint and humble deference, especially as it is relied on in cases involving state and local legislation, can rob the nation of those valid constitutional services that sometimes only the Court can perform. To be active and unchecked is to give free reign to the worst sins of commission; but to be self-restrained, were self-restraint possible, would all too easily be to substitute for those sins sure failings of omission. We should be most struck, however, not by the deficiencies of self-restraint but by its seeming impossibility in the modern age. The best literature of the legal profession, the most careful planning in presidential selections, the weighty opinions of thoughtful jurists have, more often than not, supported the idea of judicial self-restraint. They have also, it seems, not stemmed the rising tide of judicial activism one whit.

There is, moreover, no compelling logical connection between the apparent nonmajoritarian character of judicial review and the widespread demand for self-restraint. Restraint might, in fact, undermine the very reason for a body with a nonelectoral perspective in the first place. Recognizing that the United States Senate is nonmajoritarian, since senators of small states have an equal voice with those from large states, few would demand that it therefore exercise restraint in the pursuit of those functions it is empowered to perform. Similarly, to apply the rule of self-restraint to the Court may cause us to lose whatever valid function and proper contribution the Court may actively offer in the arena of American politics. The Court's value to us will be increased if it can take its place as an active but checked, not self-restrained and passive, instrument of government. And again, if the fear is that the nondemocratic element may become the antidemocratic element, ruling in place of the democracy, then calls for self-restraint will be not only inappropriate but probably ineffective. What is demanded is a way of allowing the Court to contribute to the process of democratic rule in a manner that neither minimizes its potential contributions nor gives the Court the right to rule against that democratic will which it was designed to inform.

The Complex Interaction of American Politics

"I draw my idea of the form of government," Tom Paine said in the year of independence, "from a principle in nature which no art can overturn, viz. that the more simple anything is, the less liable it is to be disordered, and the easier repaired when disordered."[37] No statement could be more at odds with the formative impetus behind the American Constitution. Complexity, not simplicity, is the most visible element in the life of American politics. Constitutionalism and limited government, federalism, bicameralism, institutional separation of powers, checks and balances on those powers by the other institutions, staggered elections, various modes of election for different offices.... The list of interactive complexities seems capable of almost endless additions. Each branch of this seemingly baroque and convoluted political system contributes something to the nation's overall well-being and also checks, at least for a time, the excesses of the other coordinates. But these are the constitutive elements of a vision of real partnership: it was the interaction of the various contributions that, it was thought, would result in the best possible public policy for the nation. "What is called union in a body politic," Montesquieu instructively wrote about the Roman republic, "is a very equivocal thing. The true kind is a union of harmony, whereby all the parts, however opposed they may appear, cooperate for the general good of society—as dissonances in music cooperate in the producing of overall concord."[38]

These dissonances, these tensions, constitute the foundations of American politics. What is needed is not an analysis of the nature and scope of judicial power that emboldens the Court's constitutional preeminence, or one that urges it to be virtuously passive or quiescent, but one that returns the Court to the intricate arena of American political life. The attempt to resolve the tensions or remove the discordant elements implicit in the ideas of judicial review, democratic power, and constitutional government overlooks the inherent and valuable complexities of constitutional politics and forsakes that overall harmony which only the interweaving of dissonant parts can produce.

2 *Judicial Review and the Rise of Constitutional Government*

In all free States the Constitution is fixed; and as the
supreme legislative derives its Power and Authority
from the Constitution, it cannot overleap the Bounds of
it without destroying its own foundation.
—SAM ADAMS

The Early History of American Judicial Review

In 1761, fifteen years before the Revolution, in the town of
Boston, James Otis delivered a speech before the Massachusetts
Superior Court. Only portions of the speech survive, and only
in the sketchy transcriptions made by John Adams. The report
is fragmentary because Adams listened more intently than he
wrote. The speech had him transfixed. "An act against the constitution is void," argued Otis, "and if an act of Parliament should
be made in the very terms of this petition it would be void. The
executive Courts must pass such acts into disuse."[1] The words

were less factual and descriptive than they were—in their muted, legal tones—revolutionary. The speech that Adams so imperfectly recorded was the first colonial challenge to the conventional idea of absolute parliamentary sovereignty. Oddly enough, Otis' words were addressed not to the king, not to the people, but to judges. He urged the judges of the Massachusetts court to set aside an act of Parliament. And it was with this speech, with this demand that judges reject a legislative act as void and "unconstitutional," Adams declared, that "the child Independence was born."[2]

The speech seemed to Adams both a warning and a prophecy. "James Otis was," he declared, "Isaiah and Ezekiel united."[3] Nonetheless, as revolutionary and prophetic as Otis' arguments may have seemed in the colonial context, the idea of judicial review was not completely new, nor was it even an American invention. Britain's Lord Coke had expressed the embryo of a similar view in *Dr. Bonham's Case* in 1610, and Coke's words were familiar to subsequent generations of jurists: "It appears in our books, that in many cases, the common law will control acts of parliament, and sometimes adjudge them to be utterly void: for when an act of parliament is against common right and reason, or repugnant, or impossible to be performed, the common law will control it and adjudge such act to be void."[4]

There was, in this view, a law clearly superior to legislative acts, a law that could overturn contrary parliamentary legislation. More important, it was a law that spoke through the agency of judges. In 1615 and again in 1702, the British chief justices Sir Henry Hobart and Sir John Holt repeated Coke's statement on the power of the judiciary, under reason and the common law, to review acts of Parliament, and Coke's dictum also found its way into the abridgements.[5]

Yet, except for *Dr. Bonham's Case*, instances of actual nullification of parliamentary laws by British courts cannot be cited. Even Hobart and Holt, in repeating Coke's words, did not act on them. Thus, if Otis' speech that day in Boston was revolutionary, it was so not because he invented the idea of judicial review but because he, a colonist, now demanded that it be applied.

Of course, Otis' request was denied. Within the British legal system—under which the Superior Court of the colony of Massachusetts was organized—the request for a judicial nullification of parliamentary legislation was almost certain to fall on barren ground. Despite the various passing mentions of judicial review in British legal circles, the power of any judge to reject acts of Parliament as void was a power that was, in British law, politically dead.

In large part the reasons for this situation are not obscure. The political climate in eighteenth-century England was hardly conducive to putting restrictions on growing parliamentary power into the hands of the king's courts. For over a century British politics revolved around the attempt to increase the power and authority of Parliament, and in that context any judicial nullification of a parliamentary act was almost predestined to fail. If the growing power of parliamentary sovereignty was in any way to be restrained, it would not be, either in logic or in politics, through the agency of royal judges. Thus, by the middle of the eighteenth century, Blackstone propounded what seemed to be the unexceptional fact of British political life:

> If the parliament will positively enact a thing to be done which is unreasonable, I know of no power that can control it; and the examples usually alleged in support of this sense of the rule do none of them prove, that where the main object of a statute is unreasonable the judges are at liberty to reject it; for that were to set the judicial power above that of the legislature, which would be subversive of all government.[6]

Despite these developments in British political theory, the American view of parliamentary power was heading in a different direction. After 1760, in the face of what appeared to the colonists as unwarranted interference with their affairs, the Americans began to formulate not defenses of parliamentary supremacy but restrictions on the exercise of parliamentary authority. During this period a full-scale revival of political and legal theorizing took place in the colonies, all of it intent on defining the true ground—and the true limits—of British political power. Under the pressures of imperial politics, Americans reexamined the nature of representation, of the social compact, and of sovereignty. As we all know, they drew up distinctions between internal and external, or direct and indirect, taxation, and they carefully reworked the then nebulous idea of a constitution. They sharpened their views on the separation of powers and severed its connection to the older notions of mixed government and the representation of estates. And, come 1776, they reformed the political structures on which to base their liberty and their security. In that decade and a half before the coming of the war, Americans were willing to consider almost any measure that promised to temper the scope and force of parliamentary legislation over their lives. Within this context it was hardly inappropriate for the colonists to revive and reformulate the dormant idea of judicial review.

This emerging colonial attachment to judicial review contained strong elements of irony. Not only were colonial judges being asked to limit that which English judges dared not restrict, but English superintendence over colonial legislation was now turned around. Britain, it could be said, had set a precedent for the colonists to follow by both claiming and exercising a type of review over colonial legislation from the very start. Although it cannot be called "judicial" review, the Privy Council and (after 1696) the Board of Trade had power to, and did, disallow acts of colonial legislation contrary to British policy. In that same capacity the Privy Council also assumed final appellate jurisdiction over colonial court decisions. Though Americans were hardly fond of such imperial oversight, they retained the principle of review as they tried to discover ways of reversing its application. With Lord Coke's theory in hand, the colonists now sought the right in turn to scrutinize and reverse parliamentary enactments.

This concept of judicial review found quick acceptance within the colonies. Four years after his speech on the Writs of Assistance, in one of the most important pamphlets of the Revolutionary period, James Otis again took up the call for judicial nullification of unwarranted parliamentary acts. The very essence of the British constution, Otis argued, was the idea of "a perpetual check and balance" of each branch of power against the others, whereby "if the supreme legislative errs, it is informed by the supreme executive in the King's courts of law." Within the theory of this balance "the judges of the executive courts have declared the act 'of a whole parliament void.' See here the grandeur of the British Constitution.' "[7] The Massachusetts House soon adopted Otis' ideas as its own,[8] and Governor Thomas Hutchinson, in denouncing that resolution, was moved to remark, "Our friends to liberty take advantage of a maxim they find in Lord Coke that an act of Parliament against Magna Carta or the peculiar rights of Englishmen is *ipso facto* void. This, taken in the latitude the people are often enough disposed to take it, must be fatal to all government."[9] The following year, in 1766, a court in Virginia unanimously declared that the "law of Parliament imposing stamp duties in America" was "unconstitutional."[10] And the same year Judge William Cushing, later one of the original justices of the United States Supreme Court, charged a jury to ignore particular acts of Parliament as "void" and "inoperative."[11]* So within five years of Otis' first prophetic oration, the idea of judicial review was alive and healthy in America, proclaimed in the speeches of patriots, in legislative actions, and in judicial opinions.

Although the idea of judicial review was clearly gaining in colonial popularity as an argument against unrestrained British power during this period, the theoretical foundations of the idea nevertheless remained rather obscure. *Why* should judges have the right to overturn parliamentary legislation? Coke had

---

*John Adams remarked to Judge Cushing, "You have my hearty concurrence in telling the jury of the nullity of Acts of Parliament" (*The Works of John Adams*, ed. Charles F. Adams [Boston: Little, Brown, 1850–56], 9:390–91).

spoken about the power of the common law or of "right and reason" to control acts of Parliament. But he offered no clear analysis of why acts of Parliament may not themselves supersede or define the common law, or why judges were the proper referees between Parliament and "reason." In 1761 Otis derived the judges' revisionary powers from the superiority of what he labeled "natural Equity" and the British "constitution." But how judges came to possess this power over the national legislature from either of those sources was not made clear. And in 1765 Otis argued for the power as a function of some type of British theory of checks and balances. Yet none of these arguments was explored in any depth. America's initial acceptance of the concept of judicial control of legislative acts seems to have developed simply from the hope for that one additional check on political power beyond the colonists' own direct control, a check that might be yet another barricade in the defense of colonial rights against imperial abuse. It was not, it seems, a concept the colonists felt compelled to explore or justify.

Partly because the theory of judicial review was only shallowly rooted and partly because the Revolution changed the context of American political life, in 1776 the unexpected happened. With the coming of independence and self-government, the American idea of judicial review fell quickly and quietly into disuse. What had seemed, superficially, to be a vital political principle in the colonial dispute with the mother country was now submerged. Americans no longer needed an intermediate check between themselves and external authority; the external authority was gone. Americans now ruled themselves. Despite its grand beginning, in the decade following the Revolution judicial review was almost as forgotten in America as it was in England.

Constitutionalism

To understand the later revival of judicial review in American politics we must now turn to the intellectual history of a related idea—the notion of "higher law" or, in more political terms, "constitutionalism." Despite the decline of the idea of judicial review with the coming of revolution and home rule, the idea of a constitution as "higher" or (to invert the metaphor but keep the sense) "fundamental" law did survive intact the coming of American independence. Back in 1610 Lord Coke had attempted to connect judicial review to exactly this concept—to the idea of an overarching set of fixed principles that would direct and govern ordinary legislation. But the failure of judicial review to take root in England is partly due to the denial that there existed such a set of British principles—such a "constitution" apart from or above the existing and changeable arrangements of laws, institutions, and customs. Then, as now, to speak of the "Constitution of Great Britain" is to refer not to a document or controlling set of principles but, at most, merely to a general description of British political life. Over that polity there is no written document, no popularly ratified description of political powers, no overarching and visible set of permanent governing principles and commands in accord with which Parliament must measure its activity. And after the Glorious Revolution of 1688 the doctrine of parliamentary sovereignty became so central to British political thought as to give to Parliament full power over elections, legislation, and even the form and character of the government itself.* Given such plenary power, there could be little room in Britain for judicial interference with supposedly "unconstitutional" acts.

But before the coming of independence, Americans had revolutionized for themselves all former notions of constitutionalism. They had rejected the belief that a constitution was

---

*James Madison would later write that, in Britain, "the authority of the parliament is transcendent and uncontrollable as well with regard to the constitution as the ordinary objects of legislative provision," comprising, as he noted, even the "full power to change the form of the government." That is, in Britain the constitution was viewed as nothing more than "a law established by the government, and alterable by the government" (*Federalist*, no. 53, pp. 360–61).

merely a description of the existing but changeable arrangements of laws, institutions, and customs. In its place they developed the notion of a constitution as a positive set of principles and rules above laws, institutions, and customs, a superior law concrete and not ambiguous, against which all other laws were to be measured.[12] The notion that the British Parliament "derives its authority and power from the constitution, and not the constitution from Parliament" (as the Swiss-American theoretician John Joachim Zubly said in 1769), or that "the power of Parliament, and every branch of it, has its bounds assigned by the constitution," had very little relation to British political fact but great impact on America's own constitutional development.[13] Americans have always shown themselves to be an inventive people—and, in politics, the idea of "the British Constitution" was an American invention of the first magnitude.

Americans found it easy to gather the insights necessary to develop this notion of a higher political constitution from their own unique history. Within the relationship of colonies and mother country the principle of superior imperial law and inferior local law was long and well established. It was on this basis, as we have noted, that the Privy Council oversaw colonial policy. Some of the colonies were of course "charter" colonies, deriving their political life and form from a "higher" document, their charters. On an even more theoretical level there was the general acceptance of the social contract as the formative impetus behind political orgnanization; and this contract took visible shape in such documents as the Mayflower Compact. Wherever Americans looked in their history, they saw evidences not of organic political growth from primordial beginnings, not a natural development from prepolitical forms, but formative acts, written beginnings, official superintendence, and limiting, binding documents.

Yet even this early history of American constitutionalism might not have persisted had it not been connected to the central theoretical truth thought out and developed in the mind of the eighteenth century. The daily colonial impressions of British imperial power and the political theory that the colonists absorbed all taught Americans an ineradicable lesson: absolute power, uncircumscribed and unchecked, all too quickly becomes arbitrary and oppressive power. Liberty demanded that limits—written limits—be placed on the exercise of all political power. The range and scope of public authority, the times and modes of election, the reserved rights of citizens—all these and more should be removed from political tampering. Public liberty, even in a democracy, depended on "the government of laws and not of men," on the security that could come only from a set of rights and principles that were not subject to the whim of the powerful. Constitutionalism—the idea of a written statement of binding principles and rules—was America's most significant, and perhaps most lasting, contribution to this goal of limited political power.

With the coming of independence every state except the old semiconstitutional charter colonies of Connecticut and Rhode Island wrote (and sometimes rewrote) constitutions for themselves between the years 1776 and 1789. And though they were, as Jefferson remarked, "new and unexperienced" in the writing of constitutions,[14] Americans could not discard the notion, which they themselves had originated and developed, of constitutionalism as "a set of fundamental rules by which even the supreme power of the state shall be governed."[15]*

Constitutionalism and Legislative Supremacy

These new state constitutions or sets of "fundamental rules" were generally written by the elected legislature of each state.†

*This idea of an all-governing constitution was surely aided by the general idea of "higher law," or laws of nature antecedent and superior to positive law, which infused the thinking of the Revolution. See Edward S. Corwin, *The "Higher Law" Background of American Constitutional Law* (Ithaca: Cornell University Press, 1928, 1955), especially pp. 72–89.

†In Rhode Island and Connecticut the state assemblies simply altered and endorsed their existing corporate charters.

None of the early state constitutions was submitted to the electorate for its approval, and in every case the body that developed the state constitution acted in a legislative capacity before, during, and after the writing of it. Soon, however, it became obvious that the writing or promulgation of a constitution by a legislative body was liable to some rather serious objections. For one thing, such a practice failed to keep distinct the simple but now crucial dichotomy between fundamental principles of law and ordinary legislation. A constitution should not be just another act of the legislature. Furthermore, since a constitution was meant by its very nature to construct the political framework of society, it was difficult to explain how a constitution could be constructed by a department of government. And finally, since that which a legislature makes it can also unmake, the very idea of a constitution seemed to demand a more secure basis than legislative fiat. As Jefferson correctly lamented in 1785, "the ordinary legislature may alter the constitution itself."[16] New Jersey, for instance, changed the wording of its constitution in 1777 by a simple legislative act. The South Carolina legislature repeatedly suspended its constitution. And the governor of North Carolina, rather than submit to a clear abrogation of his power granted by the state constitution, found himself compelled to quit his office. In the light of these difficulties, Americans began to examine and reexamine what their belief in constitutionalism actually demanded and how best to make it work. More important, the power that state legislatures had over state constitutions in the 1770s and 1780s forced Americans to think about various methods by which they could secure the idea of constitutional government and avoid devolving into the English system of simple legislative sovereignty.

The first response to this situation, however, was not a call for judicial oversight of constitutional texts against legislative power but a solution wholly American: popular conventions, distinct from state legislatures, could be given the task of formulating and promulgating the fundamental organic law for a state. The same popular will that elected the states' legislatures could first express itself in a temporary body, a convention, and give the fundamental law to the whole state, including the people's legislature.* The power to establish the fundamental law would be put in none but the people's hands. It was an ingenious method avoiding some of the theoretical and practical problems of constitution writing by the legislature.

Ingenious as it was, however, the idea of relying on such conventions could resolve only a part of the problem. Constitutions prescribe rules—what should and should not be done by law. But all rules, all constitutional directives, have to be understood, that is, they have to be "interpreted." To deny the writing of a constitution to the legislative branch is insufficient if the final power of interpretation is still to be in the hands of that same legislature. Since every American legislature (to quote Sam Adams) "derives its Power and Authority from [its] Constitution," it may not, by either outright violation or interpretive constructions, "overleap the Bounds of it without destroying its own foundation."[17] Moreover—as the town of Concord, Massachusetts, officially declared as far back as October 1776—"a Constitution in its proper Idea intends a System of Principles Established to Secure the Subjects in the Possession and enjoyment of their Rights and Privileges, against any Encroachments of the Governing Part," including, as the resolve pointedly noted, "the Supreme Legislature."[18]

*Massachusetts was again the leader in this new development. After the legislatively written constitution of 1778 was rejected by a 5 to 1 majority of towns in the state, the people of Massachusetts elected a special body of representatives "to form a Convention for the sole purpose of framing a new Constitution." The constitution proposed by that convention was adopted overwhelmingly in 1780, and in fact, though greatly amended, it still governs Massachusetts to this day. Perhaps more impressive than the longevity of the work of that convention was the fact that the Massachusetts example of writing a constitution in convention then served as the guiding model for the other states. See Gordon Wood, "Conventions of the People," in *The Creation of the American Republic* (Chapel Hill: University of North Carolina Press, 1969), pp. 306–43, especially pp. 340–41. The Massachusetts situation in 1780 is thoroughly reviewed in *The Popular Source of Political Authority: Documents on the Massachusetts Constitution of 1780*, ed. Oscar Handlin and Mary Handlin (Cambridge: Belknap Press of Harvard University Press, 1966).

It was this realization that the legislative interpretation of a constitutional text can be materially indistinguishable from legislative writing of the constitution that led Pennsylvania and Vermont to create their famed "Councils of Censors" and New York to establish its "Council of Revision" to review acts of their legislatures regarding constitutionality.[19] And finally, it was here—in the fear that state legislatures would "overleap the Bounds" the people had set for them—that the prerevolutionary idea of judicial review began slowly to reemerge as a possible check on legislative power in the later years of the period of confederation.

Thus between 1610, when Lord Coke sought to establish it, and the mid-1780s, when it began its hesitant but lasting revival, the doctrine of judicial review had a rather uneasy history. Dormant and near death for over a century, it was called, unprepared, to do battle against parliamentary legislation in the 1760s. It was relied on by patriots in the 1770s only to find itself quickly put aside as unnecessary, even unacceptable, by the same statesmen who proclaimed it as true and proper in the earlier fight for independence. Its new life in American politics grew not from any merit of its own but from its ability to lend support to that more important and established principle, constitutionalism. Review by judges was not, to be sure, the only way to support the idea of constitutionalism against the threat of legislative supremacy. But, unlike councils of censors, it had the advantage of not being entirely novel or unfamiliar. The political world had seen it before; and if it seemed weak, it at least was safe.

In theory, though not yet in practice, judicial review was a doctrine in conflict with itself. It, too, suffered from the problem of unlimited power. Once judges are set to watch the constitution and declare its meaning, who or what will restrain the judges from their own unconstitutional acts, acts against the same constitution that defines and limits all power, judicial as well as legislative? In the 1780s, however, that problem was largely theoretical. If Americans did not raise that question with any persistence, it was because, in the long, feeble history of judicial review, judges were never the villains against liberty or constitutional rights—they were always, simply, too weak.

The Tension between Constitutionalism and Democratic Government

After its use in the colonial fight against parliamentary sovereignty, the principle of judicial review grew as a possible check on the potentially unlimited sovereignty of American legislatures. In the battle between legislative supremacy and constitutional government, judicial review was easily pressed into the service of constitutionalism. But here the perceptive reader may raise a fundamental objection, one that goes to the very heart of America's ultimate but difficult acceptance of judicial review. Though it may well be true that legislative oversight of the meaning and application of any constitution can lead to legislative "tampering" with the fundamental law, nevertheless, since both the law of the constitution and the enactments of the legislative body are products of the same sovereign popular will, what possible difference can legislative interpretation make? In other words, why not let legislatures (so long as they truly are agents of the public) formulate interpretations of constitutional directives as they see fit?

Such a question is far from academic, since it lies at the base of all purely democratic critiques of judicial review. For, in the end, why should we really worry about unconstitutional legislation? Why not let the people's regularly elected representatives have full control over constitutional issues, and if the sovereign people disapprove of what was done, allow them to rectify the error at the next election? What better way is there for the people to keep the interpretation of their constitution where it rightly belongs, that is, in their own hands?

It is not a sufficient response to that kind of objection to argue that the legislature could not be trusted to carry out the public will, that it might pursue its own interests and not the public's. If that were the real problem, more frequent elections or shorter terms in office would solve it with relative ease. No, the fact is that the idea of a constitution embodies more than merely a blueprint that the people can follow in supervising their elected representatives or controlling their political leaders. Democracy, not constitutionalism, is the best means of effectively keeping executives, legislators, and legislative acts in accord with the will of the people. The full meaning of "constitutionalism," on the other hand, carries with it not only the idea of restraints on governmental action,[20] it surely carries with it also the idea of restraints on the democratic will itself.

If we wish to have a clear answer to the questions "Why judicial review? What good is it?" we have to reflect here for a moment on this fact, this generally unexamined tension in American political life. The purpose of judicial review in a democratic nation is not to keep the legislative branches true to the will of the people who elected them. Nor can its purpose simply be to keep our political representatives in line with our Constitution. If judicial review is to have substance, it must do more than that. It must also help us to bind ourselves to our Constitution.

The intriguing fact is that a democracy that did not consciously wish to bind its own will would hardly take the pains to write a constitution. Through a constitution a nation does more than merely lay out temporary constructs for elections, powers, and political procedures. The American idea of a constitution has been, as the Concord Resolves noted, "a System of Principles"—principles by which the society can weigh and measure its own activity. Constitutionalism is, in brief, a method by which the democracy purposefully guides its activity in the light of certain expressed principles, and restricts its own actions now and in the future. Constitutionalism was surely meant as a limitation on the unbridled exercise of legislative power. And by that very fact it was also a conscious limitation on the ordinary power of the popular will itself.

Within a democratic society, then, the ideal of constitution-alism necessarily embodies the idea of democratic self-restraint as well as restraint on political power—a way of holding back the popular will from casual revisions of basic political goals or from subversion of particular rights and privileges. A "consti-tution" grew to be in America a method of asserting in the present certain principles by which the democracy itself elected to regulate its present and guide its future, a way of ensuring that democratic government would be, through the years, prin-cipled government. In the final analysis, then, a constitution is more than a system of political organization or a catalogue of governmental restraints; it is that architectonic statement of laws and principles under which people bind themselves and their futures with the strongest of formal ties.

Seen in this context, constitutionalism is hardly a simple con-cept. Chapter 1 developed the argument that there is an in-herent tension between the activity of judicial review and the notion of popular government. This brief chapter has discussed the tension between constitutionalism and parliamentary or leg-islative supremacy and (in the same vein) the tension between constitutionalism and popular government itself. It is within this latter tension that judicial review gains its life and sustenance. And it is within that tension, as we shall learn, that judicial review finds its inherent limitations.

The American devotion to constitutional government made the resurrection of judicial review a possibility. Such constitu-tionalism meant, first and foremost, the checking of political power. Most obviously it meant the checking of unlimited leg-islative powers; and it was here, as a potential check on legislative autonomy, that the prerevolutionary notion of judicial review began to gain increased support. But perhaps the most signif-icant defense of judicial review under the aegis of constitutional government is not simply that it has the potential to help check the autocratic exercise of power. The highest and most complex attribute of judicial review is its potential ability to help the nation as a whole govern itself and direct its progress in the light of constitutional principles: not only principles that might need to be applied to new circumstances, but principles that—like the colonial ideas of sovereignty and equal right and even constitutionalism itself—might grow, develop, and expand. Its justification, if one is to be found, must be in that original American desire to be bound by and to live according to certain ideas and principles of just social conduct embodied in the words of a constitutional text. The underlying promise of judicial review is that with it we may bring our philosophy, our principles, to bear on our actions, and thus work out our present and our future in terms of our inheritance from the past. It was in these two roles—as the legal check on political excess and as the mediator of our principles—that judicial review once again developed.

But such roles are not unproblematic. Both are, to be sure, sharp double-edged swords: the impetus that propels the Court to be a check also demands that no branch, not even the judiciary, become autonomous or unchecked itself; and the desire to live by stated principle means that no branch, not even the Court, can reform or shape those values freely or at will. That the Court draws sustaining power from its ability to be a principled check on the exercise of power means that it, too, may be neither autonomously powerful nor unprincipled. To find a place for judicial review, to find a justification for its continued exercise, means to find a place for it within this delicate and complex system—to see it as an institutional check on power, yet as an institution that must itself be checked and watched; as an institution that is in tension with democratic rule while at the same time it has the potential to help the democracy rule itself by its own principles, that is, rule itself constitutionally.

3 The Growth
of Judicial Power

A final judgment or decree in any suit, in the highest
court of law or equity of a State ... where is drawn into
question the validity of a treaty or statute of, or an authority exercised under, the United States, and the decision is against their validity ... may be re-examined,
and reversed or affirmed in the Supreme Court of the
United States.

—1 *U.S. Statutes at Large* 73

Judicial Review before the Federal Constitution

In 1786 John Weeden, a Rhode Island butcher, refused to
accept paper bills rather than gold or silver for the meat sold
in his market. Under a recent Rhode Island law the penalty for
such refusal was harsh: anyone accused of the crime was given
only three days to prepare for trial, no jury was allowed, no
appeal from a conviction was allowed, and the fine was fixed,
steeply, at £100. As Weeden's lawyer could not reasonably deny
that his client had refused the paper scrip, he confronted the
law itself. The law under which Weeden stood accused, he argued, was unconstitutional; in enacting it the legislature had

56

overreached its legitimate powers and violated the recognized principle of trial by jury. Therefore the court—in this case the Superior Court of Rhode Island—should nullify it.

When the court handed down its decision, it studiously avoided a declaration that the questionable law was unconstitutional. The judges merely held that the case was "not cognizable" before them, and quickly dismissed the complaint. Butcher Weeden was freed and suffered no penalty despite the fact that, as everyone knew, he had openly disregarded Rhode Island's notorious paper money law.[1]

Why the case was "not cognizable" before such a court was not at all clear. But the legislature of Rhode Island was not content to let later generations of legal scholars dissect the case to explain exactly what had happened, or why the court had not held Weeden punishable under law. In their rather direct way the lawmakers declared, not unreasonably, that by refusing to enforce a clear law in a clear case the judges had "adjudged an act of the supreme legislature of this state to be unconstitutional."[2] They then sent out state sheriffs to bring the judges to stand trial before them.

To the legislature the situation was intolerable: the very judges who had sworn to apply the laws of the state against all violators had themselves acted in defiance of the law. In fact, all that stood between the judges and immediate dismissal from office was an opinion of the attorney general that strictly defined criminal offenses alone were grounds for impeachment—and the judges' conduct in this case was not, in strictly legal terms, defined as "criminal." But the lawmakers were content to fall back on an even easier punishment than impeachment: when the judicial term ended, later that year, the legislature refused to reappoint four of the renegade jurists, and replaced them with men "of a more compliant character."[3]

It was now exactly twenty-five years since James Otis had first argued the cause of judicial review in neighboring Massachusetts. And clearly, in 1786, the idea of judicial review was still in a state of flux. Yet, despite the scorn that the lawmakers of Rhode Island had for it, the idea of judicial review of "unconstitutional" legislation was slowly gaining momentum.

Such instances of judicial review in the states before the adoption of the federal Constitution in 1789 are very sparse, but those that exist are instructive. In 1784, two years before *Trevett* v. *Weeden*, a local New York City court disregarded a state law that allowed persons whose property was invaded in time of war to recover damages. Such a law seemed to the court to be in direct violation of both the international custom of nations and the recent treaty with Great Britain. The New York State Assembly, unimpressed by such arguments, passed a vote of censure on the court. But before the conflict between the legislature and the court became even more serious, the principals in the case compromised their differences and the issue faded away.[4] In a somewhat more ambiguous instance of judicial review, the Supreme Court of New Jersey had, in 1780, reversed a statute calling for six jurors in certain cases and substituted the more usual number of twelve. Despite the fact that the court's action was unclear (since other laws of the state distinctly stipulated twelve jurors and not six), the general public opinion of the day tended to regard this case—*Holmes* v. *Walton*—as a clear act of judicial review.[5] Finally, in 1787, a year after the Rhode Island Superior Court found itself so unmercifully treated by the legislature of that state, the New Hampshire legislature was confronted with a set of judicial reversals quite similar to the one handed down in the Rhode Island paper money case. This time, however, the legislature not only accepted the judgment of the court but even voted to repeal the law in question, expunging it from the books.*

*These New Hampshire cases are known collectively as the Ten-Pound Act Cases. William W. Crosskey, who is the most critical commentator on the precedential nature of all the preconstitution state cases, refers to these New Hampshire decisions as the strongest precedent for judicial review in the whole Confederation period (*Politics and the Constitution*, 2 vols. [Chicago: University of Chicago Press, 1953], 2:968–70). For another critical review of these cases, see James Allen Smith, *The Spirit of American Government* (Cambridge: Belknap Press of Harvard University Press, 1965), pp. 87–94. Compare Raoul Berger, *Congress v. the Supreme Court* (Cambridge: Harvard University Press, 1969), chap. 2.

As is usually the case with ideas at their birth, the principle of judicial review was still unclear and hesitant. The idea that state legislatures could not act tyrannically or autocratically would easily have gained common assent. But the idea that judges were the potential guardians of such legislative limitations was not yet widely admitted. The idea that no people should act beyond their constitution, in violation of their principles or against the norms of civilized nations, would have gained universal agreement immediately. But the idea that judges were properly charged with the obligation to call a recalcitrant people to task for their transgressions was as yet hardly obvious. Judges, to be sure, had every reason to be cautious in approaching the power of review. The precedents were few and weak, the arguments uncertain, and the consequences often grave. Yet, despite this mixed and clouded situation, one thing was clear: by 1787 the idea of judicial review was no longer dormant, and even its most hesitant steps elicited careful public scrutiny.*

Judicial Review and the Federal Constitution

In the summer of 1787 the Founders gathered in Philadelphia and wrote a new constitution for the United States. Given the public tension between legislatures and state judges in the previous few years, it would be unreasonable for us to think that the Founders were unaware of the legal ferment taking place around them. All of the men who gathered in Philadelphia were immersed in current affairs; their daily lives often revolved around questions of legislation and adjudication. They certainly

---

*In 1787 the Supreme Court of North Carolina held a state act "unconstitutional and void" (Bayard v. Singleton, 1 Martin 5, N.C. [1787]). The report of this case appeared in the Philadelphia papers while the Federal Convention was in session. In fact, William Davie was both a delegate to the convention and co-counsel for the plaintiff in the case. (The other counselor was James Iredell, later to be a justice of the U.S. Supreme Court.) See Berger, *Congress v. the Supreme Court*, p. 40, and Wood, *Creation of the American Republic*, pp. 460–63.

knew that the principle of judicial review, which lay rejected in 1776, had recently grown in notoriety and in strength.

But we can go even further. Within the Constitutional Convention, acceptance, not merely recognition, of this principle of judicial review was evident. It gathered strong support from all sides—from the delegates of small as well as large states, northerners as well as southerners, nationalists as well as confederationalists. Elbridge Gerry, a delegate from Massachusetts and an antagonist of the final Constitution, stated quite matter-of-factly that the "exposition of the laws ... involved a power of deciding on their Constitutionality." Not only, he added, had state judges actually "set aside laws as being against the Constitution," but they had done so "with general approbation."[6] Rufus King, James Wilson, George Mason, James Madison, Gouverneur Morris, Hugh Williamson, and Luther Martin all expressed similar views regarding the existence and propriety of the power of judicial review.[7]* "A law violating a constitution established by the people themselves," as Madison candidly stated, "would be considered by the Judges as null & void."[8] Even those few delegates who disliked the idea of a revisionary power in judicial hands—John Francis Mercer and John Dickinson, for example—"disapproved" of the doctrine, or "thought no such power ought to exist," but they hardly denied that the power already did exist and would continue to exist.[9]† In a convention often marked by rancorous debate over every issue, great and

---

*Wilson, it should be noted, was later to be a justice of the Supreme Court. Oliver Ellsworth, judge of the Connecticut Supreme Court and future chief justice of the United States Supreme Court, argued for the existence of judicial review in the new Constitution in a speech before the Connecticut state ratifying convention (Max Farrand, ed., *The Records of the Federal Convention of 1787*, 4 vols. [New Haven: Yale University Press, 1966], 3:240).

†In fact, Dickinson, after noting that no such power ought to exist, admitted that "he was at the same time at a loss what expedient to substitute." Benjamin Franklin is the only other delegate who can be listed on the anti–judicial review side, and even this statement is an extrapolation made on the basis of his antagonism not to judicial review as such but to a presidential veto and to a council of revision. See ibid., 1:109.

small, the notable fact about the doctrine of judicial review is not that many spoke of it as an established fact, but that so few ever rose to criticize it.

Still (partly because of this lack of opposition), the debates in the Constitutional Convention are of little help to us today when we try to grasp the relationship of the power of judicial review and the legislative rights of Congress or the general sovereignty of the people. There was, simply, no debate in the convention over how far judicial review extended, for what purposes it was best suited, or what boundaries could be placed on its exercise. Its existence was assumed; its scope and limits were left unexamined.

Yet this neglect of judicial review by the framers, their almost casual assumption of its existence, perhaps should not strike us as anomalous. The men at the convention began not only with a dedication to popular government and the separation of powers but a strong belief in intergovernmental redundancy, in the necessity for effective interdepartmental checks and balances. Within the convention there was significant agreement with the notion that liberty demanded not merely popular sovereignty and regular elections but the diffusion and internal institutional counterpoising of all political power. As the Founders understood it, political liberty demanded, first, the separation of powers, and second, the effective checking of the power of any one branch by that of another. Given this theory, there is little reason for us to be surprised at the Founders' acceptance of the newly reborn notion of judicial review as if it were simply another judicial function. Given the principles of checks and balances, judicial review as an internal mechanism naturally made sense.

Moreover, if each branch of this new nation was designed, in part, to oversee the others, what possible check over legislative or executive acts is there in the judicial branch other than judicial review? Some delegates to the convention, to be sure, sought to join the judicial power to the presidential veto, to amalgamate the vetoes of both of these branches into one even more formidable grand council of revision. But when the motions for such a council failed, there was little doubt that judicial review, like the presidential veto itself, survived the separation.[10]*

The Founders' easy acceptance in the convention of 1787 of the principles of judicial review has perhaps one further explanation. The doctrine of separate and checked power was a ruling idea in the convention, but as a formula it is obviously a means to an end and not the end itself. It was largely as the Preamble stated, "to Secure the Blessings of Liberty," that this Constitution and these political forms were proposed: to establish a nation dedicated to liberty, possessing sufficient restraints on power to prevent autocracy. Here again the short history of judicial review seemed to favor its quiet, even (as we noted) casual acceptance. Although judicial review might not have been a measurably pivotal factor in the history of free government, it seemed at least a responsible ally in that endeavor. Insofar as history was any guide, the record of judicial review indicated a deep regard by judges for the protection of liberty and private rights, often at great cost to the judges themselves.

Therefore, to have made a case in the convention against judicial review, to have raised questions regarding its proper boundaries within a democracy, to have asked how an illiberal spirit ruling the Court could be countered, even to have sought to define its limits in relationship to the powers of Congress and the president necessarily would have forced a person to speak in theory and to raise objections in a vacuum. Only defenders of simple democracy or unbridled legislative supremacy could object to *Trevett* v. *Weeden*, or *Holmes* v. *Walton*, or the Ten Pound

---

*Part of the reason for the failure of such a council was the fear that it might give the Court a double negative, once when it joined with the president in council and again when it sat as a court. See ibid., 1:97–98, 109, and 2:76–78. This fear of a double check in the hands of the Court was almost certainly misplaced. As Madison later wrote to Monroe, a qualified judicial negative on legislative bills in any such council "would have precluded the question of a Judiciary annulment of Legislative *Acts*" (*The Writings of James Madison*, ed. Gaillard Hunt, 9 vols. [New York: Putnam, 1900–1910], 8:406; emphasis in original).

Act Cases—and there were few such men at the convention.*
If difficult abstractions with serious practical repercussions were
to govern the activity of the convention, there was difficulty
enough in the issues of federalism, executive power, the regulation of taxes and commerce, and the length of senatorial terms
to keep even the most energetic minds busy. Though the principles that inform it are evident—a belief in the checking of
power and a devotion to the principles of political liberty—a
careful analysis of judicial review, its function and its limitation,
is absent from all of the convention debates.

Obviously, if the Founders had thought that the power of
judicial review might later be used as the bulwark of privilege
against private rights, or that it might weaken—or even unduly
work to strengthen—national political power as against local
rights, or that it would someday involve the active promulgation
of governmental activity rather than merely the checking of
questionable legislation, we then could have expected greater
clarity from the Founders and a more extensive debate in the
convention. But such notions never arose. And so discussion of
the limits of judicial review, or of the proper restraints on judicial
independence, or of the optimal relationship of judicial power
to the democratic will never surfaced. That the Founders intended judicial review is relatively clear; what they intended us
to do with judicial review is not clear.†

In summary, this and only this can be said with certainty:
The doctrine of judicial review was mentioned, repeated, and

---

*Madison, for example, called the paper money law voided by the Rhode
Island judges in Trevett "wicked and arbitrary" (Farrand, ed., *Records of the
Federal Convention*, 2:28).

†This lack of analysis of the scope and implications of judicial review may
be part of the reason that some scholars view the power of judicial review as
a later usurpation by the Court. Although the purpose of the historical analysis
in this book is to search out a coherent understanding of judicial power and
not to attempt to legitimate judicial review by references to the speeches of the
Founders, the position that the Founders disdained judicial review is almost
certainly mistaken. Judicial review may not have seemed to them an important
element in the polity (and they surely underestimated its future impact) but it
seems unlikely that they did not expect it to exist.

widely accepted in the Constitutional Convention; its propriety was assumed by many of the most influential leaders; it naturally and easily completed the circle of checks and balances, for it gave the judicial branch a check on the other departments of power; and, finally, no serious discussion of the role of judicial review, no examination of its limits, and no investigation of the relationship of judicial power to the legitimate activity of the other branches ever took place in the convention.

The Hamiltonian Defense of Judicial Review

The early *Federalist* papers mirror this situation. Hamilton, for example, mentions the doctrine of judicial review quite matter-of-factly in *Federalist* 16, assuming its existence without feeling compelled to discuss it.* It is not until Hamilton's more famous set of essays on the Court, papers 78 to 82, that judicial theory begins to receive an intensive independent investigation.

Federalist 78 speaks directly to the doctrine of judicial review. The essay is nominally about the length of judicial tenure. But in the process of defending judicial appointments "during good behavior," Hamilton presents what he also hopes to be logically persuasive analysis and defense of judicial review itself.

Hamilton's argument is complex and multifaceted. It begins by noting "the natural feebleness of the judiciary," a branch of government Hamilton characterizes as having "neither Force nor Will but merely judgment." As "the weakest of the three departments of power," the judiciary needs a means of defense against the legislature and executive.[11] The first protection is

---

*Hamilton there notes that "an illegal usurpation of authority" would require for its success "not merely a factious majority [in Congress], but the concurrence of the courts of justice, and the body of the people. If the Judges were not embarked in a conspiracy with the Legislative they would pronounce the resolutions of such a majority to be contrary to the supreme law of the land, unconstitutional and void" (*Federalist*, no. 16, p. 104). Oblique references to judicial review are also found in no. 39, p. 256 (Madison), and no. 44, p. 305 (Madison).

permanency of office. But the truly great protection of judicial right is not length of term but the power to declare laws void. Without judicial review, without the power to disregard unconstitutional laws, there would be little to prevent the erosion of what few powers the judicial branch did itself in fact possess. In this regard the power of judicial review, like the power of the executive veto, is a clear component of the principle of checks and balances. The only difference is—although Hamilton does not mention it—that the president's power is a qualified power, as his veto is potentially subject to ultimate congressional revision. Regarding the Court in this matter, however, Hamilton is silent.

Obviously, such a picture of judicial review—as the right to veto subversions of one's own granted powers—is the narrowest defense possible under the theory of checks and balances. But no sooner has Hamilton given the Court the means "requisite to enable it to defend itself against . . . attack" than he turns to a defense of judicial review as beneficial not only to the judiciary but to the polity as a whole. Here Hamilton expands the discussion from considerations of checks and balances into the broader realm of constitutionalism itself. The limitations a constitution imposes, he argues, can be preserved in no way other than through the medium of judicial review. "Without this," he adds, "all the reservations of particular rights or privileges would amount to nothing."[12] That is, without an authority *external* to the legislature, an authority clothed with the power to disregard legislative transgressions, nothing stands between legislative authority and legislative autocracy.

But Hamilton consistently dodges any serious criticism regarding the propriety of this judicial role. To the objection that judicial review implies a superiority of judicial to legislative power, Hamilton merely responds that his position "only supposes that the power of the people [whose will the Constitution represents] is superior to both." To the objection that judicial review implies a possible superiority of the judiciary to the Constitution itself, Hamilton is content to respond that such an action would be an action not of judgment but of will, and thus hardly appropriate for an institution designed to be the mainstay of a limited constitution.[13] To the objection that judicial review might invest in the Court, permanent and unelected, all the dangers he fears in legislative dominance, Hamilton is again silent. There is almost an air of incredulity surrounding these few papers—again, as if the role of judges in the scheme of republican governance was now obvious, and any questions or problems must surely be disingenuous. In a later essay Hamilton does admit the possibility of judicial "misconstructions and contraventions," but he calls the danger "a phantom"—such activity could "never be so extensive as to amount to an inconvenience, or in any sensible degree to affect the order of the political system." Lest fears of judicial supremacy go too far, Hamilton reminds himself and his readers that the Court not only checks power, it is in turn checked: if the Court encroaches on valid legislative prerogatives, there is always the power to impeach the judges. "This is alone," Hamilton mistakenly remarks, "a complete security."[14]

With that, the power of the Court in America, under the new Constitution, is launched. The opponents of the Constitution made little mention of judicial review or the proper role of judges in a constitutional democracy. The fact that the Court would have the power to nullify legislative acts had now sufficient general acquiescence and probably sufficient precedents to make judicial review a constitutional inevitability. Yet its proper role, its limits, and its relationship to democratic power or to the other branches were all still unexplored. Unlike any other national institution, judicial review came upon us as a fact before we gave ourselves the chance to mull it over in theory. The selfsame principles that gave it life—the idea of a check on political power and the desire to live in accordance with established norms and rules—these principles will, rightly, call up for investigation the scope and the limits of judicial review itself.

After the adoption of the Constitution in 1789, the power of the judiciary steadily expanded and the idea of judicial review became even more widely accepted. Since the Constitution established a tripartite division of power in the national government—executive, legislative, and judicial—with no obvious inferiority of any one branch to the others, the status of the judiciary was destined to be enhanced, and it quickly *was* enhanced. The Constitution took great pains to establish a judiciary independent of the direct control of either the legislative or executive branch. Whereas an Englishman could rightly speak of "the king's judges," as Otis did before the Revolution, Americans could not in truth speak of "the president's judges" or "Congress' judges." The justices held their tenure and support—and their powers—independently of congressional or executive will. Such factors soon gave new stature and importance to the American exercise of judicial power.

This enhanced status of the judiciary under the principle of separation of powers, coupled, after ratification, with even stronger civic appreciation of the idea of constitutional government, government subordinate to established rules and principles, soon solidified the general public acceptance of the principle of judicial review. Thus, when the Supreme Court under Chief Justice Oliver Ellsworth was called upon to decide if an act of Congress levying a tax on carriages was or was not constitutional,[15] no voices were heard either on or off the bench declaring that such a judgment was beyond judicial competence. And when the states of Kentucky and Virginia denied, in 1798, the right of the federal government to pass the infamous Alien and Sedition Acts, the responses of some of their sister states included the remark that such constitutional questions were not for the states, but for the Court, to decide.[16] So even in the earliest years of the Republic the power and prestige of the Court—and with it the doctrine of judicial review—grew and prospered. All it needed to secure its existence for good was one well-constructed case, one invulnerable decision.

Marbury v. *Madison*

The facts of the *Marbury* case are well known. By declaring a section of an act of Congress unconstitutional—an act that the

Court read as a donation of unwarranted power to the Court itself—Marshall managed to secure firmly and finally the right of review and at the same time to deflect any attempt on the part of the Jeffersonians to attack the Court itself. The opinion of the Court in *Marbury* was, of course, a political triumph. But it was also the first major judicial analysis of the theory and scope of judicial review since Coke's opinion in *Dr. Bonham's Case* in 1610. Between 1610 and 1803 the debate over judicial review took place in the speeches, pamphlets, essays, conventions, and legislative pronouncements; it was only rarely a debate joined by the judiciary itself. Yet after 1803, all debate over judicial review and the power of the judiciary in a democratic society has consistently and necessarily returned to what Chief Justice Marshall said—and left unsaid—in *Marbury*.

Marshall's arguments in *Marbury* are almost as familiar as the facts of the case themselves. Since the Constitution is superior to ordinary legislation, an act repugnant to the Constitution is void. Since it is the "duty of the judicial department to say what the law is," when two laws do conflict it is the duty of judges to enforce only the paramount law. And, finally, the courts' acceptance of congressional opinion regarding the correctness of Congress' own legislation would "subvert the very foundation of all written Constitutions," for it would not leave Congress limited in its powers but rather would invest it with both "practical and real omnipotence." Thus the supremacy of the Constitution, the nature of the judicial function, and the principle of constitutionalism all support the right of judicial review over national legislation. Marshall closed by mentioning two other sources in support of this doctrine—the judicial oath and the supremacy clause. But he merely cited them, for the case, it seems, had already been made.[17]

In the end, however, the most intriguing aspect of the *Marbury* case is not that it secured the principle of judicial review for future generations, but the way it sought to secure that power. Marshall's analysis is neither simple nor self-evident, and his logic has rightly troubled judicial scholars from the start.

Consider Marshall's arguments from the doctrine of constitutional supremacy: "If an act of the legislature, repugnant to the constitution, is void, does it, notwithstanding its invalidity, bind the courts, and oblige them to give it effect?"[18] That "an act repugnant to the constitution" is void is surely true; that its repugnancy is discoverable by judicial determination is, however, not so evident in either logic or law as Marshall seems to make it. As we noted in Chapter 2, though the principle of constitutionalism allows for the possibility of judicial review, it hardly commands it, any more than it commands the establishment of councils of censors, councils of revision, or any other particular variety of superintendence over legislative acts. Constitutionalism and limited government may be necessary conditions, but they are surely not sufficient conditions, for the exercise of a judicial veto. In fact, the real question is not, as Marshall framed it, whether an act of Congress contrary to the Constitution is valid. Of course it is not. The question is whether the power to decree its unconstitutionality lies in the courts.[19]

Marshall tried to answer that objection with a single strong rejoinder that goes far beyond the confines of constitutionalism. On that rejoinder, as we shall see, rests all of America's future problems with the exercise of judicial power. To the implicit objection "Who gave the Court the right, more than Congress, to say what is and what is not constitutional?" Marshall responded: "It is emphatically the province and duty of the judicial department to say what the law is." Despite an acknowledgment that the Court is itself "as well as the other departments ... bound by that instrument" (i.e., the Constitution), and despite an acknowledgment that the popular will is supreme (though it, constitutionally, "can seldom act"), the obvious effect is that, in matters of constitutional interpretation, Congress is bound and the Court is the body empowered to bind.[20] In Marshall's analysis, review by judges of legislative acts exists by reason of the nature of the act of judging itself, for judges have the inherent obligation "to say what the law is."

But there are some rather obvious problems with Marshall's

argument. It is questionable whether the right of judicial review can be defended by the statement that judges have the duty to say what the law is, for that statement, as it applies to the Constitution, is exactly the matter under scrutiny. Furthermore, Marshall's ontological proof for the existence of judicial review—judges say what the law is, the Constitution is law, therefore judges must say what the Constitution is—results in such a radically new extension of judicial power (for the Constitution is law in, as we have seen, a radically new and different way from ordinary legislation) that one would surely rather see it defended by some means other than by derivation from definitions.* Marshall's argument is purely formal, resting as it does on analogy and definition, and still leaves us with the question whether the Court has the right to say what *this* law, the Constitution, is.

The obvious reason to be cautious in this area is that, unlike judicial exegeses of ordinary law, law that can be refashioned at will by legislative act, the Constitution can be reshaped only by those whom Marshall declared "can seldom act," the people in three-fourths of all the states. Marshall's analysis gave to the Court the potential for extraordinary powers hitherto not present in the ordinary act of interpreting and applying ordinary legislation. When we begin with the perspective that "the Constitution is law" and add the statement that judges "say what the law is," we find ourselves perilously close to a simple acceptance not merely of judicial review but of ultimate judicial supremacy, for the Court's new power can now more easily become final power.

This last point is crucial, for the principle of constitutionalism that Marshall began with but did not pursue raised the

---

*It should be noted that, contrary to Marshall, one could with even greater propriety announce the truism that "it is emphatically the province and duty of the *legislature* to say what the law is." Consider also Archibald Cox: "It is hardly self-evident that only judges can interpret the laws" (*The Role of the Supreme Court in American Government* [New York: Oxford University Press, 1976], p. 12).

possibility, even the necessity, of checks on judicial as well as on legislative power. Conversely, Marshall's narrow legal principle that judges say what the law is gives judges wide latitude in the construction of their own powers (as was, in fact, the issue decided by the Court in *Marbury*) and does much to vitiate the idea of a constitution as a check on all branches of power. If, following Marshall, we base our understanding and defense of judicial review on the idea that "the Constitution is law," then the primacy of the Court in the American system of governance becomes more set. But if our basic view of the Constitution begins not with what the Constitution is—law—but with what it established—a constitutional democracy of separated powers, checked and balanced—then the activity of judicial review becomes part of an interlocking totality of governance. In other words, the idea of the Constitution as law interpreted by judges and the idea of the Constitution as a framework for limited government may well lead to different results.

It is part of the brilliance (if we may call it that) of Marshall's analysis that, despite his initial discussion of limited government and the demands of a written constitution, there is no evidence in this decision of any limitation on the exercise of judicial power, except for the words of the Constitution, which the Court itself interprets and applies. In a sense Marshall carefully deflected his arguments away from constitutionalism and limited government by his central argument, that judges are always empowered to say what the law is. Still, since the Constitution was meant to be, as Marshall said, "a rule for the governance of courts, as well as of the legislature,"[21] what we next need is a constitutional analysis of the limits of judicial power and an inquiry into the effective and practical checks on the Court. On that score *Marbury* is silent.

Marshall's analysis is clearly reminiscent of, even derivative from, Hamilton's defense of judicial review in the *Federalist* papers. But some of Hamilton's ingredients are missing. Gone are the remarks on judicial feebleness; gone the references to the dependence of the judiciary on the "executive arm" for the efficacy of its judgments; gone Hamilton's reference to the possible substitution of judicial willfulness ("on the pretence of repugnancy") "to the constitutional intentions of the legislature";[22] gone the recollection of the congressional power to impeach the Court; and gone, most important, Hamilton's arguments that the power of judicial review gained some portion of its existence from the theory of checks and balances among mutually coequal branches.

These observations on Marshall's arguments in *Marbury*, though they dispute the breadth of Marshall's vision of judicial powers, should not be taken to mean that judicial review itself is in any way an illegitimate or usurped power. Beyond the general support judicial review received in the convention and the explicit support it received in the *Federalist*, by 1803 judicial review had sufficient precedent in both law and public expectation to be considered an acceptable constitutional doctrine. It is rather the scope of Marshall's analysis, not the principle of review itself, that should cause us to pause. We must bear in mind that the way that the Court defends its power of review will ultimately help to determine its function in American life.

In arguing for the existence of judicial review, we can, of course, go further than attempting to reconstruct the intentions of the Founders, further than reliance on the fact that it was, by 1803, accepted and expected. Contrary to Marshall's analysis, let us examine alternative lines of argument for judicial review. Let us begin with the words of the Constitution itself.

The best evidence for the power of judicial review is in Article VI, the supremacy clause. "This Constitution, and the Laws of the United States which shall be made in Pursuance thereof; and all Treaties made, or which shall be made, under the Authority of the United States, shall be the supreme Law of the Land; and the Judges in every State shall be bound thereby, anything in the Constitution or Laws of any State to the contrary notwithstanding." Marshall mentioned this clause as "not entirely unworthy of observation," but left the analysis of it undeveloped.[23] Fully described, it would proceed as follows: First, state judges have the clear obligation to put aside the laws and constitutions of their own states which are in violation of the United States Constitution, national treaties, or valid federal law. This means that, for the first time in legal history, the power of judicial review, the power to deny effect to enacted legislation, exists not by inference or supposition but by command: the power of judges to void local laws that are in conflict with higher positive law is now enunciated in the higher law itself. In the clearest manner, the United States Constitution gives the power of review over state law directly to the judiciary of each state.

But, as Article VI also notes, not all federal law will necessarily supersede state enactments; only those federal laws made "in Pursuance" of the Constitution are to bind the judges in every state. The only place where the Constitution itself draws the distinction between valid and unconstitutional federal law is in this section addressed to the judges in each state. And just as these judges now have the power and the obligation to compare state law with the nation's Constitution, so must these judges have the ability to compare federal law with the same Constitution in order to decide (before they are forced to strike down a state enactment) whether or not the federal law is truly "in Pursuance," whether or not it is constitutional.[24] The phrase "in Pursuance thereof" clearly indicates the possibility of "unconstitutional" national legislation, and it is before these state judges that that question will first be raised.*

*Although one may argue that all duly passed federal laws are, *ipso facto*, in pursuance of the Constitution, such an interpretation seems highly unlikely. The classic statement of that position can be found in Crosskey, *Politics and the Constitution*, 2:990–95, where he contends that "in pursuance" means not "in accord with" but rather "under" or "in consequence of." Richard Funston repeats this position in *A Vital National Seminar: The Supreme Court in American Political Life* (Palo Alto: Mayfield, 1978), p. 8: "The term *a statute made in pursuance of the Constitution* may easily be interpreted to mean simply a statute properly enacted according to constitutionally specified procedures: a bill passed by Congress and signed by the president or passed over presidential veto by the required majorities in Congress." Were this interpretation to be true, to speak of a federal law as "unconstitutional" would almost always be meaningless. Such an anomalous interpretation is less easily made than it may appear to be. One could believe it only by overlooking completely the historic development

It would be impossible for state judges to exercise judicial review in cases concerning both state and federal legislation and yet for the federal judiciary, over which the Supreme Court has final authority, not to have the same power itself. The failure of such a power to reach the federal courts would undermine the constitutional decree that the federal courts' powers extend to "all Cases, in Law and Equity, arising under this Constitution [and] the Laws of the United States.[25]* In making this absolutely clear, section 25 of the Judiciary Act of 1789 expressly stated "that a final judgment or decree in any suit, in the highest court of law or equity of a State . . . where is drawn into question the validity of a treaty or statute of, or an authority exercised under, the United States, and the decision is against their validity . . . may be re-examined, and reversed or affirmed in the Supreme Court of the United States."[26]

A second defense of judicial review could be inferred not from the constitutional text itself but from the very structure of the national government. In view of the careful and deliberate, almost mathematical, coordination of powers and checks devised by the Founders, it would be exceedingly anomalous

---

in America of the idea of limited government or of constitutionalism itself and by assuming that, in one unpublished step, the Founders jettisoned any real restrictions on political activity at the national level and reestablished the idea of complete parliamentary sovereignty in an American disguise. Still, we need not argue the point that far. Despite Crosskey, the Founders meant by "in Pursuance" exactly what common sense would indicate. Consider Hamilton's exegesis on the phrase in *Federalist* 33. There, acts that are "not pursuant" are acts not against specified procedures but against substantive limitations. Hamilton offers such examples as a federal law on descents or interference with state property taxes. Such acts are "invasions" or "usurpations," and not to be considered as the supreme law of the land (pp. 206–7). In this context "in Pursuance" surely means much more than simply "according to constitutionally specified procedures."

*The reason behind this power to review lower state court decisions is obvious. "Confidence," as Madison observed in 1787, "cannot be put in the State Tribunals as guardians of the National authority and interests. In all the States these are more or less dependt. on the Legislatures" (Farrand, ed., *Records of the Federal Convention*, 2:27–28; see also Madison's speech of July 5 in ibid., 1:124).

for the third branch of the government to have no effective revisionary control over the actions of other coordinate branches. The legislature, divided in two, has a check on each side; the presidency has its check on the legislative power (notably the veto), while the Congress can balance out that check under certain situations (most notably its power to override). The principle of separation of powers, on which the structure of the national government is built, implies that "each department," as Madison remarked, had "the necessary constitutional means, and personal motives, to resist the encroachments of the others."[27] Each department must possess, again in the words of the *Federalist*, "a constitutional control over the others."[28] But what "constitutional" means of control over the legislature or the president could the judiciary have aside from the then familiar one of judicial review? As Jefferson himself put it, "the Judicial power ought to be distinct from both the legislature and the executive, and *independent* upon both, that so it may be a check upon both, as both should be checks upon that."[29]

Though all commentators feel compelled to note that *Marbury* is a masterpiece of political maneuvering whereby Marshall raked from the ashes of a hopeless and embarrassing situation the power of review in such a way as to leave his adversaries without effective challenge, what is generally left unnoticed is that he sought to secure this right not with the best of arguments but with less compelling ones. This, too, is impressive. Yet if Marshall did use less than the tightest of constitutional logic, it may well be because the sounder arguments, though they might have conceded to the Court the right of review, might also have admitted other ideas as well. Consider the two alternative arguments made above. The first, the supremacy clause, to which Marshall made only passing reference, though it would ultimately have vested the power of judicial review in the Supreme Court, points far too clearly to the states (in the persons of their own appointed judges) as also proper investigators of the legitimacy of national law. And the second argument, from the equal coordination of power, not only would have ended by granting the Court its check on the two remaining branches but also would have served to emphasize those branches' coordinate checks on the Court. Moreover, such an argument would have aided another major contender for the post of official interpreter of the Constitution, namely, each coordinate branch. Both of these modifications of or additions to judicial review—state review and the equality of legitimate interpretation by each branch—would soon be strongly defended by the very person the decision in the *Marbury* case was aimed against: Thomas Jefferson. Clearly, what Marshall needed was not the best arguments that would allow the Court judicial review, but arguments that would set off the Court as, in Marshall's words, the "especial," the "emphatic" interpreter of the organic law, the interpreter capable of binding all states and all branches. *Marbury* v. *Madison* does more than secure for the Court the power to check legislation as part of an interlocking system of mutual checks and balances. It carefully lays the ground for the more problematic position that the Court is the final and supreme authority on all matters constitutional.

The infancy of judicial review was now over. The power of judges to nullify legislative acts, invoked, then discarded, by partisans of varied causes over the years, had now found itself defended by the judicial department itself. Because of John Marshall, the coming task would no longer be to sustain its life but to employ its services while restraining its potential excesses: to have it guide but not control democratic life; to have it apply but not revise the Constitution; and to have it work with, not over, the coordinate branches of national political power.

4 *From Judicial Review to Judicial Supremacy*

> In the State Constitutions and indeed in the Federal
> one also, no provision is made for the case of a disa-
> greement in expounding them; and as the Courts are
> generally the last in making the decision, it results to
> them by refusing or not refusing to execute a law, to
> stamp it with its final character. This makes the Judici-
> ary Department paramount in fact to the Legislature,
> which was never intended and can never be proper.
> —JAMES MADISON

The great salutary effects of *Marbury* should not be mini-
mized. In that decision Marshall secured the principle of judicial
review for future use, reasserted the primacy of the Constitution
as both a permanent and adaptable document, and—by por-
traying the Court as a watchdog over all constitutional infractions, large or small—raised in the public's estimation the
legitimacy of all judicially accepted national legislation in a new
and vulnerable Union. During Marshall's tenure these promises
bore fruit in the great expansive readings given to national
power in *McCulloch* v. *Maryland* and *Gibbons* v. *Ogden.*[1] Without
Marshall's sure insight and persuasive reasoning in those cases,

the Constitution's vision of a great and unified nation might well have been rejected.

But with the principle of judicial review also came the danger of a judiciary, as Madison put it, "paramount in fact" to the other branches of politics and to the national will itself. Argue as one may that the doctrine of separate powers was not meant by the Founders to bring about the political primacy of the judicial branch over the coordinate departments or that the doctrine of constitutional supremacy was not meant to establish the supremacy of judges, the truth is that the doctrine of judicial review soon did allow the Court to stamp both legislation and the Constitution "with its final character." Having connected its judgment to the mandates of the Constitution, the Court acquired for itself the dangerous potential to rule finally, even imperially, over both the popular will expressed in law and, more serious, over the people's Constitution itself. And it has been exactly that problem—what to do about a Court superior to democratic politics and final in its constitutional decrees— that has so often challenged the minds of statesmen, jurists, and scholars alike. This chapter discusses the two most comprehensive critics of judicial power in American history: Jefferson, who sought to erode the power of review, and Lincoln, who sought to discover ways of mitigating its unwarranted and potentially harmful effects.

Jefferson and the Democratic Alternatives to Judicial Review

As long as Jefferson thought that the courts would be adequate barriers to despotic legislation, he spoke out firmly and clearly in support of judicial review. As we have already seen, part of Jefferson's original argument in favor of attaching a Bill of Rights to the Constitution was that it would enable the courts more easily to reject illiberal national legislation. "In favor of a declaration of rights," he wrote Madison, is the fact that it would put "a legal check [on repressive legislation] . . . into the hands of the judiciary."[2]

Yet, with the failure of the courts to void the Alien and Sedition Acts of 1798, Jefferson retreated from his optimistic view of judicial liberality. Both this experience and his later presidential conflicts with the judiciary led Jefferson to formulate various other devices for constitutional interpretation. The first of these devices may be described as state review, the second as coordinate or departmental review. Although neither is fully satisfactory, through them we may see even more clearly the limits of judicial review itself.

State review of federal law involves a position that history usually describes under the heading of "nullification." Jefferson, with Madison, formulated the doctrine in quick response to the Federalist Alien and Sedition Acts, passed under Adams' administration. The position begins with exactly the principle Marshall used in *Marbury*: "Whenever the general government assumes undelegated powers, its acts are unauthoritative, void, and of no force." Whereas Marshall derived from this fact the revisionary power of the courts, Jefferson turned not to judges but to the "creators" of the Constitution—the states. As the states had ratified the constitution and given it life, they could authoritatively declare, within their borders, the meaning and application of the document they created. The Constitution was a "compact" among the several states, a compact within which, as Jefferson said, "each party has an equal right to judge for itself, as well of infractions as of the mode and measure of redress."[3]

Jefferson was probably correct in seeing the Alien and Sedition Laws as contrary to the constitutional powers of Congress. And he was also correct in noting that his original hope—that the judiciary would become the barrier of liberty against power— had been far too sanguine. Still, state review, as an alternative to review by the courts, must be counted as among the least attractive of possible contenders. In the context of a nation, and not a mere confederation of sovereignties, Jefferson's idea of state review finally reduces itself to a necessary contradiction. To seek "sovereignty in the Union and complete independence in the members," as Hamilton remarked, is "to aim at things repugnant and irreconcilable."[4] Even Madison—who was Jefferson's colleague in the Virginia and Kentucky Resolutions that enunciated this position—later admitted that "the final appeal" on matters of constitutionality "must be to the authority of the whole not to that of the parts separately." Any other arrangement, he declared, would make for "a government in name only."[5] As a substitute for judicial review of federal legislation, state review poses more problems than it solves.

Jefferson's second doctrine, that of departmental review, does indeed refer decisions on constitutionality to the authority of the whole and not to the states. It begins with the principle that Hamilton used to buttress the idea of judicial review in the *Federalist* papers, the principle that *Marbury* was to downplay— that of departmental equality and independence. To Hamilton, it will be recalled, political liberty required that "the power of judging be . . . separated from the legislative and executive powers."[6] Hamilton, of course, derived from this fact not only the right of the judiciary to use the power of review to defend its own prerogatives but to use its power to nullify laws whenever the Court held that the Constitution was breached. But to Jefferson, if liberty required the separation of powers, it also required that each branch must be independent of, rather than subservient to, the interpretive views of any other. The legislative, the executive, and the judicial powers inhere, by constitutional command, in separate departments, and the powers of one branch cannot be undermined or subverted by the interpretation given the Constitution by any other branch.

Jefferson did not claim, as a result, that each branch can simply interpret the Constitution as it wills. Rather, he held that each branch must construe the Constitution for itself *as it concerns its own functions.* As Jefferson wrote to Abigail Adams, he considered it his duty as chief executive, under "the obligation of an oath to protect the Constitution," to refuse to enforce "the pretended sedition law." "I considered," he argued, "that law to be a nullity, as absolute and as palpable as if Congress had ordered us to fall down and worship a golden image; and that it was as much my duty to arrest its execution in every stage, as it would have been to have rescued from the fiery furnace those who should have been cast into it for refusing to worship the image."[7] Thus the Court has no more authority to tell Congress or the president what the Constitution meant in establishing congressional or executive power than the Congress or the president has to tell the Court what the constitutional duties of an independent judiciary entail. Any attempt by Congress to interpret for the Court the constitutional prerogatives of the Court—to demand, for instance (to use an example from *Marbury*), that a court make one witness sufficient for a conviction of treason—would be an act that the judiciary could properly leave unenforced. As concerned its own functions, the Court was independent and supreme. And by the very same principle, Jefferson argued, the Court cannot interpret, for the Congress, the meaning of Congress' legislative prerogatives or delineate for the presidential office what the Constitution meant by the grant of executive power.

Jefferson's defense of this rule of interpretation rests on two grounds, the first constitutional, the second democratic. The Constitution, as Jefferson noted, intended "to establish three departments, co-ordinate and independent, that they might check and balance one another." But to give "to one of them alone the right to prescribe rules for the government of the others" would have the effect of consolidating the greatest political authority in that single branch, thus uniting in one department exactly what the Founders had tried so hard to separate and check. Second, not only was the institutional interaction of checks and balances essentially subverted by the doctrine of complete judicial oversight, it was subverted by that branch which is, in its very foundations, "unelected . . . independent of the nation," and "seriously anti-republican." "A judiciary independent of a king or executive alone," Jefferson admitted, "is a good thing;

but independence of the will of the nation is a solecism, at least in a republican government." And, given the fact that judges are not angelic but only human—that "they have, with others, the same passion for party, for powers and for the privilege of their corps"—their independent authority and secure tenure, when added to the doctrine of judicial review over all branches, makes the institution a serious contradiction within a democratic country.[8]* This consideration is, of course, a partial restatement of our original problem—how properly to combine democratic republicanism with an enduring legal document that binds the republic—and Jefferson's answer denies the propriety of setting apart a body of people as the authority by which a democracy is bound to its own designs.

Jefferson's analysis reminds us again of some of the serious theoretical problems faced by the doctrine of judicial review, especially by any understanding of judicial review that implies the supremacy or finality of judicial decisions in a constitutional democracy. Still, his own doctrine of coordinate review suffers from equally grave limitations, both theoretical and practical. Jefferson is, for example, particularly imprecise in helping us determine which branch of government a question is properly before. Why, for example, would the question in *Marbury* (concerning a judicial appointment by the president under congressional law) more properly concern presidential rights than judicial prerogatives or congressional intent? And who would decide? Furthermore, on the level of basic constitutional theory the position seems contradictory—we intended (to use Jefferson's words against him) to establish not only three "coordinate and independent" departments, but coordinate and independent departments that would "check and balance one another." But if each branch could absolutely and with finality decide for itself the

*Consider the note Madison appended to the debates in the Federal Convention of 1787 for Tuesday, July 17: "An independence of the three great departments of each other, as far as possible, and the responsibility of all to the will of the community seemed to be generally admitted as the true basis of a well constructed government" (Farrand, ed., *Records of the Federal Convention*, 2:36).

bounds of its own power, where would be the checking? Or, to place Jefferson's understanding within the framework of a more contemporary practical critique, what would have been the result of Jefferson's theory of final coordinate constitutional interpretation in the Watergate crisis?*

Jefferson ultimately saw the political difficulties inherent in the idea of separate departmental interpretation and he was willing, later in his life, to entertain the notion of one authoritative instructor of constitutionality, one branch that could by right settle questions of constitutional meaning. But this branch, he continued to argue, should not be the judiciary. A judiciary "independent of the will of the nation" and "secured against all liability to account" was the only one of the three branches capable of real constitutional despotism.[9] It was Congress, not the judiciary, that should have the "exclusive authority to decide on the constitutionality of a law." Rather than leave final constitutional interpretation in the hands of each separate department or in the several states, Jefferson was now most willing to consider the idea that "the legislature alone is the exclusive expounder of the sense of the Constitution, in every part of it whatever."[10] Such a view combines the political security of having one final constitutional authority together with the theoretical advantage of contributing to democratic rule. Or, to argue Jefferson's point further, in a democracy there seems to be, at least on its face, greater justification for legislative or even executive authority over the sense of the Constitution, since the decision of those political branches is subject to popular referendum, and that of the judiciary is not.

Attractive as Jefferson's position may seem, it is subject to

*One of the more interesting consequences of final coordinate interpretation is that it radically increases the power of the president over the other two branches. Under it a president could, for example, refuse to execute laws passed over his veto and upheld by the courts, thus changing his qualified veto into an absolute one. Or he might refuse to execute long-standing legislation on the grounds of constitutional scruples. (See Robert Scigliano, *The Supreme Court and the Presidency* [New York: Free Press, 1971], p. 16.) In this light the reader should consider Jefferson's statement to Abigail Adams, quoted above.

exactly the same objection that was raised in Chapter 2: legislative review overcomes, denies, that salutary and important
tension between constitutionalism and democratic government.
To make the Congress the exclusive expounder of the Constitution is tantamount to a rejection of what we have described
as one of the earliest American developments in constitutional
theory, a development grounded in the belief that the Constitution should remain out of the legislature's making (for interpretation is a vehicle—as Jefferson noted regarding the Court—
for, *sub silentio*, remaking). Congressional review supports one-
half of the tension between constitutionalism and democracy—
democracy. It minimizes the relevance of a constitution as a self-
binding of the democracy upon itself and it blurs the distinction
between the Constitution and ordinary legislation. We might
also note that, in a practical sense, the difficult and complex
system of constitutional amendment would thus become merely
a superfluity. To the degree that this is all true, Marshall was
unambiguously correct: popular review (for this is what congressional review reduces itself to) is close to no limited constitution
at all. A way must be found to preserve, even perhaps to increase, congressional authority in the area of constitutional
interpretation without resort to the position that Congress should
be the exclusive authority on matters constitutional.

Nevertheless, this survey of Jefferson's views is important,
for in them we have a compendium of all of the various radical
alternatives to judicial review—state review or nullification, coordinate review, and, finally, legislative (or, in a sense, popular)
review. Not that these alternatives are simply failures, for each
of them encompasses an important part of the American constitutional structure. And each of them, while limited, clearly
points out some of the difficulties of judicial review itself. But
they all suffer from the defect of oversimplification; an oversimplification that, if adopted, would have overcome the tension
between constitutionalism and democracy by blinding us to the
historic and proper reasons behind that tension.

What is needed is not any alternative to judicial review but rather a way of preserving judicial review while preventing judicial supremacy. What is needed is a way to keep all parts of this three-cornered tension alive—to preserve judicial review, constitutionalism, and democracy together. Jefferson understood the problems involved here and sought to resolve the tension in favor of the superiority of the democratic will. Our purpose must be more complex and difficult—to keep democracy, constitutionalism, and judicial review in a supportive and complementary relationship to one another; that is, to keep the tension in balance, not to resolve it.

Despite the attacks of Jefferson and Jeffersonians on the Marshall Court, the legitimacy of judicial review in American political life very quickly took deep root. Moreover, much to Jefferson's chagrin, the power of judicial review not only was accepted, it soon began developing into the doctrine of judicial finality—the belief that, on matters of constitutional correctness and constitutional error, the Court's word is equivalent to the authoritative, final word.

As we saw in Chapter 3, even before *Marbury* the Federalist-dominated legislatures in the northern states responded to Jefferson's and Madison's Kentucky and Virginia Resolutions with the reply that the "ultimate" and even "exclusive" determination of constitutionality was vested in the Court.[11] After *Marbury* this doctrine of judicial finality, the belief that the Court through its decisions on constitutional questions sets for the nation the meaning of the Constitution, began to take on all the aspects of constitutional orthodoxy. When Andrew Jackson, for example, vetoed the Bank Bill of 1832 because of constitutional scruples, Daniel Webster denounced the president's act as illegitimate. The Court, Webster noted, had declared such banks legitimate in *McCulloch* v. *Maryland*, and no official could refuse to treat that view as authoritative and binding. An opinion of the Court regarding the meaning of the constitutional text, Webster said, is "final, and from [it] there is no appeal."[12]

This doctrine of judicial supremacy, though denied by Jackson in the bank dispute and rejected by Jefferson throughout his career, had sufficient practical and theoretical plausibility to recommend it to a wide cross section of the American people. In a nation deeply troubled by regional and sectional conflicts, the idea of a final interpreter of the Constitution's mandate within the central government itself seemed rather favorable to the forces of American nationalism. Moreover, to have a single authoritative expositor of the nation's law seemed (at least in theory) to take the most explosive issues of the day out of the electoral arena and settle them more objectively, in the interest of general peace. From almost the beginning of the Republic the judges of the Court were endowed by popular myth with the attributes of dispassion and disinterest; who better, then, to decide the meaning and commands of America's fundamental legal text? And though particular pieces of state legislation were disallowed, fully half a century would pass before the Court would void an act of national legislation as it did in *Marbury*. Obviously to have argued seriously about the dangers inherent in judicial finality in the early years of the nation might well have earned one the title of speculative philosopher removed from actual political fact. Without any but the most theoretical reasons to question it, the doctrine of judicial review took on all the attributes of a doctrine of judicial supremacy. So when the Court declared, finally and authoritatively, in its second exercise of judicial review, that no political power could stop the expansion of slavery in the territories and that the right of whites to own blacks was "a right distinctly and expressly affirmed in the constitution," fully half the nation was thrown into utter turmoil.[13]

Abraham Lincoln and the Limits of Judicial Supremacy

"I tell you," Stephen Douglas said with calculated smugness to Lincoln in the sixth of their debates, "that I take the decisions of the Supreme Court as the law of the land, and I intend to obey them as such."[14] Douglas had every right to be smug, for the Court had elevated his attack on the Missouri Compromise to the level of a constitutional command. In *Dred Scott* v. *Sandford* the Court officially declared that the extension of slavery into the western territories could not be prevented by either Congress or the territorial legislatures, that freed Negroes could not be citizens or enjoy the constitutional privileges of citizenship, and, almost gratuitously, that the national dedication to the natural equality of all men meant, in fact, only the equality of some men. The Court's authoritative interpretation—from whose opinion (Douglas declared) "there is no appeal"—was that the right of whites to the possession of property in a slave was "a right distinctly and expressly affirmed in the constitution."*

The questions decided by the Court in *Dred Scott* were hardly idle exercises in logic or law. Upon the ability of slaveholders to colonize the growing West lay the whole future of slavery. The question that had so deeply split the country now seemed to be resolved: the Court denied the nation any power to stop the spread of slavery into new lands. In only its second formal exercise of judicial review over national legislation, the Court showed the intrinsic problem with the cavalier equation of judicial decisions with the official, final teaching of the Constitution itself. And it was that decision—on which the whole future

---

*Justice Peter Daniel was even more blunt. The federal government, he argued, has a "direct obligation . . . to protect and *enforce* . . . the property of the master in his slave," as slaves are "the only private property which the constitution has *specifically recognized*" (19 Howard 393 [1857], concurrance, 490; emphasis in original). The Court's declaration through Chief Justice Roger B. Taney that the right to possess property in a slave is "distinctly and expressly affirmed in the Constitution" lends strong support to Lincoln's claim that the judicial resolution of the divisive issue of slavery would be to nationalize the institution (*The Collected Works of Abraham Lincoln*, ed. Roy P. Basler [New Brunswick, N.J.: Rutgers University Press, 1953], 2:461–69, 3:78–95, 100, 230–31, 250–51). The reading of substantive protection into the due-process clause of the Fifth Amendment, which Taney did in *Dred Scott*, would have worked to preserve slavery in the District of Columbia; and the supremacy clause, Art. VI, sec. 2, would have worked to prevent the constitution or laws of any state from destroying the right of property in a slave, a right defined as "distinctly and expressly affirmed in the Constitution" of the United States. The reader is directed to the citations in Lincoln noted above for the complete development of the argument.

of a race and a nation depended—that Lincoln and Douglas debated in the year 1858.

The oddest aspect of those parts of the Lincoln-Douglas debates concerning the nature of the Constitution is that our popular contemporary ideas of judicial review are always expressed by Douglas and never by Lincoln. "It is the fundamental principle of the judiciary," Douglas said in the third debate, "that its decisions are final. It is created for that purpose so that when you cannot agree among yourselves on a disputed point you appeal to the judicial tribunal which steps in and decides for you, and that decision is binding on every good citizen."[15] "The Constitution," Douglas further declared, "has created that Court to decide all Constitutional questions in the last resort, and when such decisions have been made, they become the law of the land."[16] "Whoever," therefore, "resists the final decision of the highest judicial tribunal, aims a deadly blow to our whole Republican system of government—a blow which if successful would place all our rights and liberties at the mercy of passion, anarchy and violence."[17] It was Douglas' position that in regard to questions of constitutionality, the Supreme Court's word is authoritative, controlling, and final.

Although Douglas was a political descendant of Jefferson's Democratic party, he was, in these arguments, hardly a descendant of what Jefferson considered his own more democratic spirit. To Jefferson the solution to the problem of judicial autocracy was to minimize the role of the Court in constitutional matters—to heighten the freedom allowed the more immediately popular branches or to augment the power of the democracy itself. To Stephen Douglas the solution to all constitutional questions was finally and absolutely in judicial hands—the Court's decisions were, simply, the law of the land. The only matter of constitutional interpretation on which, it seems, Jefferson and Douglas agreed was the desirability of simplifying the problem.

To Lincoln the status of judicial authority in a constitutional democracy was considerably more complex. Dogmatic solutions that either heightened the power of the Court to direct the policy of the nation or solutions that reduced the power of the Court to insignificance were equally erroneous. Questions both of constitutional theory and of feasible policy animated Lincoln's arguments in the debates: what may we do, and can we do, about the Dred Scott case?

Unlike either Douglas or Jefferson, Lincoln began by seeking an answer to the problems of constitutional interpretation which would neither deny the rule of the people and their elected representatives in the face of judicial determinations, as Douglas tended to do, nor deny the judicial function or the legitimacy of judicial review. For Lincoln the whole task was to find a practical way of keeping judicial review alive while at the same time enlivening and not depressing the democratic nature of the polity or the constitutional powers of the other branches. That is, he sought to find ways of working within the tensions and ambiguities of American politics and not to resolve those tensions.

That the case was determinative of the legal fate of Dred Scott himself Lincoln would not deny. "In so far as it [the Supreme Court] decided in favor of Dred Scott's master and against Dred Scott and his family," Lincoln declared, "I do not propose to disturb or resist the decision."[18] All judicial decisions are necessarily binding on the parties in litigation, as well as on the executive branch for whatever enforcement is necessary. At no point did Lincoln argue, as Jefferson had done, that he would judge for himself what laws or decisions he as president would or would not enforce.* Although Lincoln learned much from

---

*Consider Jefferson's defense of his actions in the Sedition Act crisis:

In the cases of Callender and others, the judges determined the sedition act was valid under the Constitution, and exercised their regular powers of sentencing them to fine and imprisonment. But the executive determined that the sedition act was a nullity under the Constitution, and exercised his regular power of prohibiting the execution of the sentence, or rather of executing the real law, which protected the acts of the defendants. [Jefferson to George Hay, June 2, 1807, in *Writings of Thomas Jefferson*, 11:214]

Jefferson and quoted him freely, he never defended Jefferson's position that each branch was the final determiner of the constitutionality of the acts within its sphere. Rather:

> I do not forget the position assumed by some that constitutional questions are to be decided by the Supreme Court, nor do I deny that such decisions must be binding in any case, upon the parties to a suit, as to the object of that suit, while they are also entitled to very high respect and consideration, in all parallel cases, by all other departments of the government. And while it is obviously possible that such decision may be erroneous in any given case, still the evil effect following it, being limited to that particular case, with the chance that it may well be overruled, and never become a precedent for other cases, can better be borne than could the evils of a different practice.[19]*

Lincoln, in brief, never repeated the idea behind Jackson's reputed remark that "John Marshall has made his decision, let him enforce it."† But he did refer to Jackson's refusal to be

---

Although the discretionary pardoning power of the executive made Jefferson's actions uncontrovertible, clearly Jefferson denied effect to these decisions on the basis of a constitutional understanding wider than his pardoning power. "I considered it [the sedition law] as a nullity wherever I met it in the course of my duties; and on this ground I directed *nolle prosequis* in all the prosecutions which had been instituted under it" (Jefferson to Gideon Granger, March 9, 1814, in ibid., 14:116; see also 11:43–44, 12:289–90, and 15:214).

*Circumstances might, of course, make it highly imprudent or impossible for the executive to enforce every determination in each case. Lincoln did in fact ignore the wartime writ of Chief Justice Taney issued on circuit in Ex parte Merryman (17 F. Cas. 144 [1861]). But Lincoln purposely avoided raising to the level of theory what he found himself forced to do by circumstance. The best analysis of the constitutional complexities involved in Lincoln's action in this case is in Scigliano, *Supreme Court and the Presidency*, pp. 34–44.

†The phrase is "reputed" as there is no evidence to prove it, despite its currency. In fact, contrary to Jefferson, Jackson took pains to point out that the authority of the Supreme Court does not necessarily bind the executive when he is acting in a "legislative" capacity—that is, proposing, vetoing, or signing legislation (James D. Richardson, ed., *Messages and Papers of the Presidents* [Washington, D.C.: Government Printing Office, 1896], 2:582). That interpretation implies, however, that a Court decision in a case binds the president when he acts in his *executive* capacity.

bound, in his official acts, by the Court's opinions or by the constitutional principles it had enumerated.

> It is maintained by the advocates of the bank [Jackson wrote] that its constitutionality in all its features ought to be considered as settled by precedent and by the decision of the Supreme Court. To this conclusion I cannot assent. Mere precedent is a dangerous source of authority, and should not be regarded as deciding questions of constitutional power except where the acquiescence of the people and the States can be considered as well settled.[20]

Each decision of the Court, though it may set precedent, does not set policy. To both Jackson and Lincoln the issue was not the Court's authority in any particular case; its power there was unquestioned. The issue was the supremacy of the Court on matters of constitutional principle, the degree to which the Court sets with authoritative finality those principles determinative of future public policy. That is, to what degree is it true that the Constitution necessarily is whatever the Supreme Court says it is?

In Douglas' opinion—that is, in the generally orthodox opinion—an interpretation of the constitutional text enunciated by the Court is itself the supreme law of the land, and that supreme law is then binding on the other branches. Douglas and his followers, Lincoln pointed out, "would make [every such decision] a rule of political action for the people and all departments of the government"; that is, every interpretation enunciated by the Supreme Court "becomes [in Douglas' words] the law of the land, binding on you, or me, and on every other good citizen, whether we like it or not."[21]

For Lincoln's response to this position we should refer again to his First Inaugural Address:

> The candid citizen must confess that if the policy of the government, upon vital questions affecting the whole people, is to be irrevocably fixed by decisions of the Supreme Court, the instant they are made, in ordinary litigation between parties, in

personal actions, the people will have ceased to be their own rulers, having, to that extent, practically resigned their government into the hands of that eminent tribunal.[22]

Were Douglas correct, that the decisions of the nation's judges are, in themselves, the law of the land, then any resistance would be revolutionary. Were the textbook understandings of the Court as the constant bulwark of our liberties, the support of our democracy, and the guardian of our constitutional text all true, then all resistance would be worse than revolutionary: it would be senseless. Without doubt, the judiciary often has a capacity to deal with matters of theory and principle beyond that possessed by either legislatures or presidents, a capacity that would potentially enable courts and judges to be the "pronouncers and guardians of our values."[23] Yet, despite whatever truth may be contained in those observations, it is not unwarranted for us to be cautious, even critical, of judicial formulations of constitutional theories and commands. For Lincoln and for us, simple reverence for the Constitution (as well as for the Court) requires that we not believe that the Constitution is all the things the Supreme Court has sometimes claimed it is.

Let us proceed even further and consider the following: Despite our often immediate response that the Court is final and authoritative in constitutional interpretation, we have no problem with Jackson's veto of the Second United States Bank as, in his view, unconstitutional, even though a unanimous Court had already declared exactly the opposite. Nor would it strike us as anomalous if Congress rather than the president had denied passage to a bill on constitutional grounds despite prior and clear judicial pronouncements of constitutionality. Nor, to carry the point further, do we generally object to Congress' attempts to pass bills in the face of a previously negative constitutional ruling on the same topic and grounds—witness the New Deal's legislative response to the Court's prior rulings of unconstitutionality. Despite our sometimes sloppy contemporary rhetoric, if the Court is the final interpreter, it is final for us in a very ambiguous way.

The first of those examples, Jackson's veto of the United States Bank on constitutional grounds in direct opposition to the Court's unanimous opinion, involves not the president's refusal to enforce a judicial decision in a particular case but the president's refusal, before the passage of a law, to be bound by another department's reasoning regarding the meaning of the Constitution. Similarly, the New Deal acts involved not the president's enforcement of laws declared unconstitutional but the attempts of the president and Congress to force the Court to reconsider and reverse many of its prior decisions of unconstitutionality. This much should be clear: none of these examples denies the power of the Court to bind authoritatively in a particular case; all merely declare that a particular decision of the Court need not be taken as a generalized or permanent decision. They declare that judicial opinions need not be seen as the last word in constitutional construction or as themselves determinative of future public policy. And they also declare that the other independent departments of national power—the more explicitly democratic branches—have a rational and proper interest in actively shaping constitutional meaning with the Court, and often, properly, in disagreement with the Court.

The argument inherent in these political actions is part of the thesis of this book—that constitutional doctrine and constitutional interpretation are not the domain only of the Court but properly the function of all branches in active dialogue and political interaction with each other. Or, to put it another way, the genius of the American constitutional system is not merely the separation of functions but their interactions, their debates, their perennial clashes.

We can summarize and expand on Lincoln's position as follows: Lincoln affirms that, unless we purposefully wish to be revolutionary, the Constitution is the ordinary and proper instrument of American political rule. But he denies that the Constitution is equivalent, either in logic or in fact, to whatever it is that the Court declares it to be in its opinions. There is, for Lincoln, no problem in saying that the Court can be wrong about

the Constitution—and, as in *Dred Scott,* seriously and danger-
ously wrong.* The position does not claim that a judicial holding
in a case as regards the litigants can be disregarded. That path
destroys the legal process itself and reduces the whole of judging
to insignificance. But the Lincolnian position does begin with
the notion that all parts of the political process—the democratic
branches as well as the courts—have a legitimate hand in shaping
the meaning of the constitutional text. In a political system of
three independent and politically equal branches there is no
reason to assume that Court opinions are, "the instant they are
made," definitive and binding on the whole system of government. That is, judicial decisions, though "entitled to a very high
respect and consideration," need not be understood as immediately and in themselves binding as "rules of political action."[24]

Let us buttress Lincoln's claim further: one obvious problem
with the Jeffersonian notion of congressional interpretation is
that the powers of Congress are defined and limited. To lodge
immediate and final interpretive power in congressional hands
is to invite abuse. As Marshall correctly noted, to have no oversight over legislative acts undermines the very spirit of constitutionalism itself. But it is equally important to note, as Marshall
also pointed out in a different context, that "the framers of the
Constitution contemplated that instrument as a rule for the
government of *courts,* as well as of the legislature."[25] Or, as Bickel
noted, "The Constitution does not limit the power of the legislature alone. It limits that of the courts as well, and it may be
equally absurd, therefore, to allow courts to set the limits. It is,
indeed, more absurd because courts are not subject to electoral
control."[26] But what may not be absurd is to argue that final
constitutional interpretation is not the ultimate domain of any

---

*That the Constitution can be misinterpreted is of course true, even though
opinions may differ as to what constitutes a misinterpretation. To say otherwise
is to deny the whole basis of review in the first place. And to deny that the
Court can misinterpret the Constitution would put us at odds with every Court
that sought to overturn the errors and misconstructions of previous decisions.

one branch but is properly the concern of all branches, judicial, executive, and legislative.

Lincoln knew that America was deeply devoted to the rule of law, to judicial review, and to an independent Court. What he also knew was that America was a nation in which the people were to rule over all the instruments of political power and not be ruled by them or by any one of them. He knew, in other words, the implicit tension in America's devotion to both judicial review and democratic government. He knew that political liberty depended in large measure on the separation of political power and on interdepartmental checks. But he also knew that such a principle implied that the Court must exist within the framework of mutual checks, not above it. Finally, he also knew that America was a nation governed by a Constitution, a Constitution that the judiciary could—and, in the case of *Dred Scott*, did—mistake. Given this situation, the central question became how to keep judicial review as part of a system of checks and balances within a constitutional democracy; or, to put it bluntly: What checks are there on an errant Court?

"To consider the judges as the ultimate arbiters of all constitutional questions," Thomas Jefferson noted, is "a very dangerous doctrine, and one which would place us under the despotism of an oligarchy."[27] This analysis has begun with the potential truth of that danger—the danger to the nation of a Court held by theory to be uncheckable in constitutional interpretation. The analysis so far has endeavored to lay out the theoretical framework of the discussion. The following chapter will attempt to speak somewhat more practically.

5 "From This Court There Is No Appeal"

> The opinions of the supreme court, whatever they may be, will have the force of law because there is no power provided in the constitution that can correct their errors or control their adjudications. From this court there is no appeal.
>
> —ROBERT YATES

Constitutional government meant the chance to be guided by chosen principles and orderly procedures rather than to be ruled by immediate desire or by force. Through constitutionalism we placed limits on both our political institutions and ourselves, hoping that democracies, historically always turbulent, chaotic, and even despotic, might now become restrained, principled, thoughtful, and just. So we bound ourselves over to a law that we made and promised to keep. And though a government of laws did not displace governance by men, it did mean that now men, democratic men, would try to live by their word.

If we ask the question with which we began this investigation, "Why judicial review?" we can now give at least a general re-

sponse: To remind us of our ends, to permit the Court to think
through with us our principles, and to help us apply our spoken
word in law to the turning paths of change and circumstance
and event. Judicial review is not, as we have seen, an indispen-
sable part of constitutional governance; any number of constitutional republics in this world have denied such a power to
their courts. But with judicial review we hoped to increase the
possibility of living our political life constitutionally—that is, with
due reflection on and respect for the principles that bind us
together as a nation. Thus the great promise of judicial review
is that with it we may rise to the level of our highest aspirations
and live, politically, a principled life. Hamilton may have un-
intentionally misled us by saying that the Court possessed neither force nor will but "merely judgment," for in this context
judgment is hardly trivial, hardly "mere."[1] We separated the
powers of political life into different departments, giving to
some the care of discerning our present needs and desires, and
to the Court the charge of reminding us of our enduring civic
principles.

Through the dialogue and interaction of these branches
America attempted to reconcile both permanence and change,
to join together both principle and necessity. Since the Court
was to possess our best judgment, it was hardly improper for it
to have some revisionary power over the branches of politics.
As a body that would help to infuse political life with greater
reflection, the Court could realize its promise only if it could make
its voice heard and heeded in politics, if it could enter the arena
of checks and balances.

Having entered that arena, however, it must enter it fully.
Since no branch, no institution rules in America by right, no
single political institution is in itself final. The noblest task of
the Court—to be the element of thoughtfulness and judgment
within the hurried concerns of a democratic polity—should not
diminish our awareness of the dangers of judicial supremacy or
the potential fallibility of the Court as the reasoning element.
Because even the Court can mistake the nature of our binding

principles, and because the Court can often be wrong about the relationship of its vision to the pressing needs of a democracy in a complex and changing world, the Court must itself be part of, and not above, the dynamic interaction of American politics.

It subtracts nothing from the greatness of the Court to argue that its proper place is within the system of checks and balances rather than beyond or above it. To say that the Constitution was placed in its hands is not to say that the Court is the final or only interpreter of our abiding concerns or that its understanding is, or should be, beyond dispute. To argue that it is the branch best suited to explain to us our goals is not to argue that it will not be wrong, often seriously wrong. To know that it was set apart from the fleeting desires of the democracy is not to pretend that it is by right insulated from the important needs and permanent interests, or the effective power, of the democratic people. The Court is, and should be, neither all nor nothing in the political and social health of a living country. What we need is both a theory and a practice that allow the Court to exercise its potentially valuable services yet restrain what Hamilton, referring to the antifederalists' attack, described as the "errors and usurpations" that may develop from the exercise of judicial power.[2] We must, in sum, discuss ways of preventing the power of constitutional interpretation from becoming the power to rule.

We deal here not in absolutes, but in points along a continuum. The power of judicial review serves great purposes, and the reduction of that power to insignificance would be a telling loss. But to be cavalier about the increasing directive power of the judiciary in our daily social and political life or to be unconcerned about possible grave errors of judicial judgment because of our belief in judical independence would be equally dangerous. Were the fears of the antifederalists true—that "from this court there is no appeal"—there would be something radically defective with the political arrangements of a nation that sought not only to make the people rule justly and rightly but also, in the end, to justify the right of the people to rule.

Checks and Balances

All branches of American national politics were given separate tasks, then purposely checked. The accumulation of governmental power in any one branch—the combined power of legislating, judging, and enforcing one's decisions autonomously—Madison called "the very definition of tyranny."[3] The greatest danger to the security of liberty would be the potential ability of any person or set of persons to exercise substantial political power independently. So, to contain all political power within bounds, the Founders tried to do two things simultaneously. First, they took great care to separate the exercise of political authority into three functionally distinct departments, legislative, executive, and judicial. But they also took care to blur the edges of each department, giving to each some partial oversight, some partial control over the activities of the coordinates. Separating the exercise of power, dividing up the whole of political authority, was not enough to protect liberty. It was, as Madison declared, "essential to a free government" that each of these separated departments also be "connected and blended, as to give to each a constitutional control over the others."[4] That is to say, all branches of American political life were given distinct, separate tasks, then checked. By separating the departments we freed each of them from the absolute control of any other branch. But by interdepartmentally checking the powers of each branch we sought to prevent such separation from turning into the autocracy of any part.

It is the particular genius of America's understanding of republican government that political powers can be delegated by the sovereign people not only because the people have ultimate control over their officials but because their officials have themselves some effective agency in watching, weighing, and controlling the various activities of one another. Subjecting the activity of all politics to the final oversight of the people was one method of ensuring that no organ of American political life would act autonomously, that is, without responsibility. But the more immediate method of preventing independent activtity was through the balancing, the checking of each department, one versus the other.* The Founders understood, as we do, that effectively unchecked powers are intrinsically fearsome, dangerous to all rights and to all security. It was that "Constitutional control,"[5] that oversight and ability to check, in the hands of each branch, the coordinate departments of power, that would be the internal political guarantee of free government. Again to refer to Jefferson's original statement in favor of judicial review: "The judicial power ought to be distinct from both the legislature and executive, and independent upon both, that so it may be a check upon both, as both should be checks upon that."[6] It was this blending and checking of power within the structure of the government that would allow the sovereign people to go about their daily lives and endeavors securely, without the need for absolute vigilance or constant elections or perpetual daily oversight over every branch and department power.

But when Madison says in *The Federalist* that the Constitution has "distributed and blended" the powers of the various departments, we hesitate. Checks and balances seem fine in theory, but highly suspicious when applied to the Court. Our immediate reaction to most notions that assert positive external constitutional checks on judicial power is to counter with another equally noble phrase: the vital importance of an "independent judiciary." When it comes to the Court we often believe in the constitutional principle of separation of powers, of the Court's independence, but not in the concomitant constitutional principle of checks and balances as that principle might apply against

---

*The great security against a gradual concentration of the several powers in the same department, consists in giving to those who administer each department, the necessary means, and personal motives, to resist encroachments of others.... The constant aim is to divide and arrange the several offices in such a manner as that each may be a check on the other" (*Federalist*, no. 51, p. 349).

the Court. In the American mind the principle of checks and balances often stops at the door of the Court.

Reflection, however, should persuade us that all political independence is allowable only within certain limits and under certain restraints. The independence of each branch, as Madison remarked, does "not mean that these departments [executive, legislative, and judicial] ought to have no *partial agency* in, or no *controul* over the acts of each other."[7] "Complete independence and separation between the three branches," as the Court itself has said, was neither "attained or intended.... The independence of each is qualified and is ... subject to exception.[8]* And although a degree of independence is necessary to preserve the principle of separation, complete independence would indicate the kind of irresponsibility that the principle of checks and balances sought to prevent. Nevertheless, although the proponents of judicial review have no hesitation in affirming the existence of a judicial check on the other branches, they seem to become uneasy at the thought of direct reciprocal checks on judicial acts, especially in the area of constitutional interpretation. To most Americans not only is the Constitution law, but the words of the judges are, with uncontrovertible finality, the words of the Constitution.

As we have already noted, when it comes to the Court and its power of review, the temptation is always to oversimplify. The tradition that developed from Jefferson's thought has sought to reduce the effective power of the Court over the democracy by overemphasizing the supreme power of the popular will, the sovereign power of the states, or the prerogatives of Congress. The fear of judicial autocracy led Jefferson to minimize the potential value of the Court almost to insignificance, to reduce its effective place within the scheme of checks and balances. The opposing and more prevalent view begins with the notion of

---

*Consider Alexander Bickel: "Our government consists of discrete institutions, but the effectiveness of the whole depends on their involvement with one another" (*The Least Dangerous Branch* [Indianapolis: Bobbs-Merrill, 1962], p. 261).

judicial independence and ends by again removing the Court from the system of checks and balances. Unlike Jefferson's view, however, this position finds itself without defenses against the dangers and the reality of judicial imperialism.

Contrary to those views, this book seeks to elucidate a theory of judicial power in a constitutional republic on which a middle path of action might be developed. What is needed is a defense of the principle of judicial review within a system of reciprocal checks. It must be a position that recognizes and encourages the exercise of judicial review. But it must also be a position that understands the tenuous connection between judicial review and republican government. Moreover, it must be a position that understands the potential dangers to a constitutional republic— that is, government that is both principled and limited—arising from a corps of permanent judges working under notions of independence equivalent to judicial autonomy and judicial finality.

The establishment of separation of powers and interdepartmental checks and balances was meant to do two things: to ensure both the separate independence of each branch and the public responsibility of each branch. It was meant, for example, to permit presidential vigor yet to allow the nation the means to deflect an imperial presidency. It was meant to preserve legislative independence yet to help protect the nation from legislative despotism. In like manner the conjunction of separate powers with interdepartmental checks was meant as a way to guard the viability of judicial power yet to prevent judicial supremacy.

The Doctrine of Judicial Finality

It remains true, however, that the common public and academic opinion of judicial power today firmly supports a rather simple doctrine of judicial finality, a notion that the Court is, in brief, the last word in constitutional government, that its constitutional activity is not to be checked or externally restricted. This position necessarily assumes that, while the activities of the president and the Congress are reviewable by the courts, the Supreme Court's activity of constitutional construction is properly sheltered from the reciprocal oversight of the other branches. It is the doctrine of finality—the belief that, in fact, "from this Court there is no appeal"—and not the doctrine of judicial review per se that lies at the base of our concerns over judicial supremacy or imperialism.

This doctrine of finality is hardly a new understanding of the scope of judicial power. As we have already seen, this principle was present in the early Federalist arguments against the Kentucky and Virginia Resolutions, in Stephen Douglas' position against Lincoln on *Dred Scott*—in fact, one can find this view repeated throughout our history by many of those who have the Court on their side of any strongly contested issue. But, more important, we can find this doctrine of judicial finality urged upon us—perhaps increasingly urged upon us—by the Court itself.

Marbury v. *Madison* solidified for the Court the authority to declare void those acts it believed contrary to the Constitution. But Marshall's decision, while noting that the Court is in an "especial" position to pronounce constitutional interpretation,[9] did not declare that the judiciary was the only or the final interpreter of the constitutional text. Such positions are, as we have already noted, quite plausible extrapolations from Marshall's reasoning; but they are, nonetheless, extrapolations. Yet, with or without Marshall's aid, the temptation for the judiciary to see itself as final—"supreme in the exposition of the law of the Constitution," as the Court recently termed itself—is a greatly attractive temptation.[10]

"We are not final because we are infallible," goes Justice Robert Jackson's oft-quoted aphorism, "we are infallible because we are final."[11] "While unconstitutional exercise of power by the executive and legislative branches of our government is subject to judicial review," Justice Harlan Stone once remarked, "the only check on our own exercise of power is our own sense of self-restraint."[12] And, in recent memory, the Court attempted to raise up this doctrine of judicial autonomy to the highest level, to the level of a constitutional command: in *Cooper* v. *Aaron* the Court solemnly asserted that *Marbury* "declared the basic principle that the federal judiciary is supreme in the exposition of the law of the Constitution, and that principle has ever since been respected by this Court and the Country as a permanent and indispensible feature of our constitutional system. It follows that the interpretation ... enunciated by this Court ... is the supreme law of the land."[13]

This doctrine of ultimate judicial supremacy over the nation's organic law, the notion that judicial interpretations are equivalent to the Constitution itself, is a doctrine the Court would have us believe is historic, respected, and venerable.

The Fallibility of Finality

Historic, respected, venerable ... and highly problematic. Reflecting back on the analysis in the previous chapter, we will recall that just as it may seem logically absurd for Congress to have the final say over its own powers, it is equally absurd for the Court, itself bound by the Constitution, to have final interpretive supremacy over the constitutional text. There is no reason why placing interpretive supremacy in judicial hands is philosophically or practically better than leaving it in congressional hands. To paraphrase Marshall's analysis of congressional power in *Marbury*: it would be giving to the Court a practical and real omnipotence with the same breath that professes to restrict its power within narrow limits.[14]

If Congress can mistake the meaning of the text, which is what the doctrine of judicial review asserts, so, of course, can the Court. And if it be said that it is more dangerous to have interpretive supremacy in the same body that directs the nation's public policy—that is, Congress—then (especially in this age of pervasive judicial direction of political and social life) an independent judicial interpretive power is equally fearsome for exactly the same reasons. Or more fearsome, since, as we have noted, there is at least one quite obvious check on congressional power—the people and the power of their franchise—but effective checks on the power of the judges are fewer and significantly more difficult to use.* It is no longer possible, nor was it ever really possible, to get the Court out of politics and public policy. For that very reason what we need is a theoretical and practical base on which to oversee the Court as the Court itself oversees Congress and the president. That, in essence, is what the principle of checks and balances demands.

As Lincoln clearly saw, to say that the Court's interpretation of the constitutional text immediately takes on the absolute supremacy of that text itself is to violate not only the central meaning of democratic government but the whole American hope for shared and limited political power. One noted constitutional scholar, echoing Lincoln, has written:

> Judges do, of course, have a special duty to say what the Constitution, and law in general, mean, for those who apply the law to particular cases must also explain it; and so great deference is owed to the pronouncements of the judiciary. But judges are neither infallible nor the constitutional superior of Presidents and congressmen. Nor do they, in consequence, have the power to fix the meaning of the Constitution the moment they speak out.[15]

---

*Congressional supremacy, it must be added, has the further advantage of generally being able to work only through compromise among competing interests. Judicial decrees can be as narrow and ideologically partisan as they are nondemocratic. Legislative politics in America surely has real and significant defects, but a propensity to rule in an absolutist manner is rarely one of its hallmarks. The same cannot be said of institutions that do not govern on the basis of pluralism and compromise. Although the reader should be open to the limits of congressional rule which will be taken up in later pages of this book, the reader should also keep in mind the arguments made in chap. 1 regarding the generally nonrepressive nature of congressional government. Compare Ely, *Democracy and Distrust*, especially pp. 101–4 and 145–79.

To say the opposite—that the Court does, through its opinions, fix the meaning of the Constitution—is not only to declare the supremacy of judicial opinion over the democratic will, not only to declare the superiority of judicial activity to the principle of checks and balances, but to contradict the very thesis of constitutionalism—that is, restrained and limited government—itself.*

In this context, consider the blanket statement made by the Court in *Cooper* concerning judicial supremacy over the constitutional text. It seems impossible to reach the conclusion *Cooper* propounds—that Supreme Court interpretations are themselves "the supreme law of the land"—without admitting the awkward premise that the Constitution is what (or whatever) the justices care to say it is.† Were the Court's dictum there to be true, Marshall's fear of congressional power would have to be directed

---

*"The idea that a pronouncement of unconstitutionality by the Court fixes the meaning of the Constitution as against the national legislative power, though an inescapable inference from the Hamiltonian *juristic* conception of judicial review, has never assumed sufficiently authoritative shape to put it beyond the reach of important challenge" (Edward S. Corwin, *Court over Constitution* [Princeton: Princeton University Press, 1938], p. 82). "The Court is . . . obliged as a creature of the Constitution not to overstep its bounds or exceed its constitutional authority. To argue otherwise would be to say that the Court is above the Constitution or that the Constitution is a judicial supremacy document which it patently is not" (George W. Carey, "The Supreme Court, Judicial Review, and Federalist Seventy-Eight," *Modern Age* 18 [Fall 1974]:377). "While professing to be controlled by the Constitution, the Supreme Court does, as a matter of fact, control it, since the exclusive right to interpret necessarily involves the power to change its substance. This virtually gives to the aristocratic branch of our government the power to amend the Constitution, though that power is, as we have seen, practically denied to the people" (J. Allen Smith, *The Spirit of American Government* [Cambridge: Belknap Press of Harvard University Press, 1965], pp. 97–98).

†The argument would be as follows:
  1. The Constitution is the supreme law of the land.
  2. The Constitution is what the Court says it is (interprets it to mean).
  ∴3. "The interpretation [of the Constitution] enunciated by this Court . . . is the supreme law of the land."

The questionable second premise is necessary in order to reach the Court's stated conclusion. Justice Felix Frankfurter's remark bears repeating here: "The ultimate touchstone of constitutionality is the Constitution itself and not what we have said about it" (Graves v. O'Keefe, 306 U.S. 466 [1938], 491–2 [concurring opinion]).

at the Court itself: "then written constitutions are an absurd attempt, on the part of the people, to limit a power in its own nature illimitable."[16] The proper response to any doctrine of judicial supremacy is to point out that it was not only legislative omnipotence that the Founders feared, but the omnipotence— or supremacy, or finality— of any single branch, unchecked by any other. And the final doctrinal blow to the principle of constitutional government comes if we hold that, though Congress and the president are bound by the Court's interpretation, the Court itself is not.*

Restricting Judicial Supremacy: Amendment

To the question "What can we do to restrain judicial supremacy or reverse a decision of the highest Court?" the usual answer is, for any particular case, "Amend the Constitution." Because of its currency we should examine that proposition most carefully.

The first and most obvious problem with the position that only by amending the Constitution can we restrain judicial activity is that such a method is hardly a practical way to respond to any political decision, judicial or otherwise. If we take amendment of the Constitution to be the only method of calling the Court before the bar of public sentiment, we have gone extremely far toward the liberation of unchecked judicial power. Revision of the nation's basic structural document was, pur-

---

*So far we have concentrated on the problems that the idea of judicial finality faces from the perspective of legal and constitutional theory, but we could raise more purely logical objections as well. For example, are all of the varying, even conflicting, decisions of the lower federal courts (which receive the same constitutional grant of judicial power as the Supreme Court) also "the supreme law of the land"? And what shall we make of the "derelicts of constitutional law" (as Philip Kurland has called them), such as Schechter and Panama Refining, which forbade powers Congress now exercises, but which the Court has never overruled? See Philip Kurland, *Politics, the Constitution, and the Warren Court* (Chicago: University of Chicago Press, 1970), pp. 116, 185–87.

posely and properly, made a task of substantial difficulty. So the response that the only proper means of changing a Court decision is to amend the decision out of existence gives the Court a very free hand to shape and reshape politics in America.

It should be clear that there is no judicial decision, apart from the almost utterly unacceptable, that cannot find the support of a small minority able to block most attempts at amendment. Without a war and the rigors of Reconstruction, *Dred Scott* could never have been overturned by amendment, given the fact that slavery was honored by a strong, though minor, regional interest. Nor could the Court's holdings on child labor, minimum wages, or the right of the government to aid a depressed economy have been overcome by such a method. It took only a small minority, for example, repeatedly to defeat all attempts to overturn judicial support for child labor by constitutional amendment.

It should be noted that this practical objection to the necessity of amending the Constitution in order to reverse the Court has a theoretical foundation: a written constitution was meant to restrict the autonomous exercise of political power. But the conventional opinion that demands we revise the Constitution before we can change a judicial interpretation reverses that principle, for it effectively makes the Constitution the shield and security for exactly that kind of autonomous political activity we sought to protect ourselves against. We would never admit the argument that the president can, under his oath to support the Constitution, issue directives that can be reversed only by amendment of the Constitution. We would hold that opinion to be perverse, because it uses the very document written to restrict power as a barricade to protect its uninhibited abuse. The same perspective should enlighten us about the relationship of judicial power and the amending procedure.

But there are other problems with the use of the amending procedure as a response to judicial decisions. Such a position only serves, for example, arbitrarily to reinforce one type of nondemocratic activity with another. It says, at least potentially, that national policy can be reversed by the Court, and that that reversal can be kept in force simply by a small sympathetic minority. All that is needed to support a Court decision and block any attempts to amend is a negative vote in thirteen of our ninety-nine state legislative houses—a minority of 13.1 percent.

To recognize this fact is not to argue that America should change its character from a limited constitutional democracy to a pure majoritarian democracy. It is true, of course, that America is a restrained rather than a pure democracy. But to argue that the least democratic political institution can use its powers to govern and direct the polity unless reversed by the one process least available to that democracy, amendment, is to reconstruct the idea of restrained democracy into something merely arbitrary. It would be to argue in favor of exactly that which the Founders thought they had overcome, the institutionalization of minority rule.*

Needless to say, the actual effective minority does not have to be as small as 13.1 percent to cast into doubt the notion that only through amendment should a Court decision be changed. The Constitution was made difficult to amend in order to prevent precipitous changes and to deflect innovations not widely supported throughout the country. But the difficulty of amendment was not meant to protect a political or judicial decision that itself might be a radical departure, or unsupported by a wide constituency, from reversal. In simple terms, the amending process was meant to ensure that every major political change would have deep and wide support; it cannot be turned into an argument in support of policies made and protected by the smallest of national minorities. Such a method might, at times,

---

*The cool and deliberate sense of the community ought, in all governments, and actually will, in all free governments, ultimately prevail" (*Federalist*, no. 63, p. 425). *Federalist* 58 describes majority rule as "the fundamental principle of free government," and Hamilton, in *Federalist* 22, calls the ultimate reliance on majority, not minority, rule "the fundamental maxim of republican government" (pp. 397, 139).

be an "additional shield to some particular interests, and another obstacle generally to hasty and partial measures," as Madison wrote concerning all varieties of minority vetoes. "But these considerations are outweighed by the inconveniences in the opposite scale. In all cases where justice or the general good might require new laws to be passed, or active measures to be pursued, the fundamental principle of free government would be reversed. It would be no longer the majority that would rule: the power would be transferred to the minority."[17]

Moreover, despite the wide and pervasive political effects a decision may have, not every political decision should become a matter of *constitutional* politics. The aim of establishing a government of broad, but separated and checked, powers was to be able to avoid returning to the people, in their sovereign constitutional capacity, to resolve various current political disputes. Most political questions should be handled in politics. If we are to respond to judicial directives regarding the direction of public policy, we should not respond with the impractical and unpersuasive idea of constitutional amendments.*

One last point. It must be noted that amending the Constitution as the only means of reversing or modifying a judicial

---

*The defenders of the position that only through amendment can a judicial interpretation be externally reversed usually also find themselves insisting that the Constitution should not be burdened with small particulars, that it should stand generally intact and unchanged. This latter view is persuasive, for nothing would do greater damage to the very essence of the Constitution as a statement of broad and lasting principles than to burden it, dilute it, with narrow amendments responding to diverse judicial interpretations. But to couple that insight with the argument that amending is the only way to restrain the judiciary goes a long way toward an absolute practical defense of judicial supremacy. In truth, we should not want to revise our basic organic document every time the courts announce problematic decisions. The purpose of a constitution was to establish broad directive principles; it was not meant to be weighed down with particular statements adopted in response to particular judgments. Questions, for example, about busing, about reporters at pretrial hearings, about school prayers, about whether fetuses conceived by rape or incest are to be granted the same protection (or lack of it) as others before birth, about the hours or ages at which it is inappropriate for children to labor—none of these issues should be raised to the level of permanent constitutional definition.

decision is open to an obvious logical difficulty—that amendment is itself subject to final judicial interpretation. This is hardly
a debater's argument, given the fact that the three Reconstruction Amendments (13–15), passed in part to secure forever the
reversal of the holding and spirit of *Dred Scott*, were soon made
shadows of their true selves by adverse Supreme Court interpretations. Those amendments hardly prevented the Court in
the nineteenth century from subverting the amendments' manifest intent of aiding the Negro race and expanding congressional power into a haven for unregulated business, a hindrance
to national legislation, and a burden on the newly freed slaves.
The same might also be said of the judicial interpretations of
the Eleventh Amendment regarding state immunity and the
early interpretations of the Sixteenth Amendment, establishing
an income tax—both passed to reverse previous Court decisions.
If a solution to the problem of judicial supremacy is to be found,
we should begin by examining the political process itself, looking
to the foundation notion of checks and balances, and not attempt
to go outside that system.

In summary, the position that holds that the judiciary sets
the authoritative meaning of the Constitution, binding on the
nation and all branches, until the Court either reverses itself or
is reversed by amendment, converts what Hamilton called "the
weakest of the three departments of power" into potentially the
most powerful, the least checked. It is a position that greatly
increases the unimpeded independence of the Court, it arbitrarily buttresses our least democratic institution with our least
majoritarian process, and it potentially reverses the Founders'
hope that the Constitution would be difficult to change by giving
shelter to almost all acts of judicial revisionism. It is a nonserious
and impractical means of checking judicial activity.*

---

*Indeed, the more pervasive the judiciary becomes in directing public pol-
icy, the more impossible it becomes to restrain its decisions solely through the
amending process. Or, as Sam Ervin once observed, "You can't pass constitutional amendments fast enough to control the Court" (Committee on the
Judiciary, Subcommittee on the Separation of Powers, 90th Cong., 2d sess.,
Hearings, June 11, 1968,] p. 26).

Restricting Judicial Supremacy:
The Doctrine of Judicial Self-Restraint

Recognizing the inadequacy of the amending process for reviewing judicial decisions, many of the best minds in legal theory have developed and proposed a different restriction on the scope of judicial activity, namely, the doctrine of judicial self-restraint.

The principle of self-restraint begins by recognizing the vital role the Court can play in the governance of the American polity. It begins with the altogether correct premise that the Supreme Court exists to do more than merely decide cases; its grandest function is to think and reason with the polity on the best application of our highest principles to our common, present, and pressing concerns.* But the advocates of restraint also recognize that America is a nation governed not from on high but democratically, and that the Court is, of all our institutions, unquestionably the least democratic. And, finally, the advocates of restraint begin with the knowledge that while the Court can often help us see ourselves and our principles more clearly, the Court is also not preserved from error regarding the meaning, development, and application of those ideals.[18]

If we grant those premises—that the Court, as an appointed and life-tenured body, exists in real tension with democratic rule, and that the Court can do not only great good through its wisdom but also great harm through its mistakes—then judicial self-restraint becomes a seemingly reasonable answer to the problem of judicial supremacy. Recognizing the Court's awkward situation, the advocates of restraint urge the Court to decide great issues incrementally, developing those techniques that will, quite often, keep our judges from grand or speculative decisions made either in haste or in a vacuum. Finally, whenever possible, the Court should defer to the judgment of the people expressed legislatively, recognizing full well the perils of judicial

*The Court is, as Alexander Bickel has written, "the institution best fitted to give us a rule of principle" (*Least Dangerous Branch*, p. 261). This position and its limits will be discussed more fully in chap. 6.

willfulness and pride. Properly fearful of giving the Court the last word, the partisans of restraint ask it to keep a bit more silent.*

But the proponents of judicial self-restraint seem to find themselves forever fighting an uphill battle. All too often such restraint seems to be nothing less than unwarranted hesitancy to correct errors and evils that only the forceful exercise of judicial power can remedy. "Whenever," Hamilton remarked, "a particular statute contravenes the constitution, it will be the duty of the judicial tribunals to adhere to the latter, and disregard the former."[19] "We have no more right to decline the exercise of jurisdiction which is given," Marshall noted, "than to usurp that which is not given."[20] And beyond the Court's legal obligations to decide cases before it, we have an almost intuitive notion that the judiciary has something to contribute to the healthy governance of the nation, and that judicial self-restraint, rigorously applied, seriously minimizes the possibility of that contribution.†

---

*In its extreme form the doctrine would have the Court reject only those laws in which the legislature had made a clear mistake.

> The validity of the law ought not then to be questioned unless it is so obviously repugnant to the constitution that when pointed out by the judges, all men of sense and reflection in the community may perceive the repugnancy. By such a cautious exercise of this judicial check, no jealousy of it will be excited, the public confidence in it will be promoted, and its salutary effects be justly and fully appreciated. [James B. Thayer, "The Origin and Scope of the American Doctrine of Constitutional Law," *Harvard Law Review* 7 (October 1893):142]

The doctrine of the clear mistake receives its full development in ibid., pp. 144–55.

†It should be noted that Hamilton did not stop with calling upon judges to declare statutes unconstitutional "whenever" they contravened the Constitution. In a rarely noted section of the same paper he also stated that judges should not only void unconstitutional acts but "mitigate the severity" and "confine the operation" of "unjust and partial [though not unconstitutional] laws." This judicial "firmness" (as he called it) in turning back the "spirit of injustice" is "calculated to have more influence upon the character of our government, than but few may be aware of." And "whatever will tend to fortify that temper in the courts" should be prized by considerate men of every description (*Federalist*, no. 78, p. 528). Such statements hardly make Hamilton the stalwart patron of judicial restraint that some people consider him. For the contrary opinion, see Carey, "Supreme Court," pp. 356–68.

That the Court should be careful in its use of the power of review, respecting precedent and respecting the dignity and aims of lawmaking bodies, no one would deny. Judicial activism understood as the liberty of judges to act on their own desires and personal views, is unquestionably indefensible. But fear of judicial supremacy does not necessarily lead to the argument that the Court should therefore be reluctant to exercise its basic constitutional function within the system of checks and balances. Hestitant use of judicial power does not solve the problem of judicial supremacy, it merely reduces the instances, and the benefits, of judicial review. Or, to put it differently, although restraint implies the sparing and modest use of the revisionary power, restraint alone is still no assurance of its wise use. After *Marbury* the Supreme Court went over fifty years without overturning a single act of national legislation. Yet, despite such impressive restraint, the very next reversal was *Dred Scott.**

We can begin, however, by putting aside all the arguments regarding the desirability or liability of judicial restraint. The most striking thing about such self-restraint is its almost inevitable futility. One need not have a Hobbesian view of man as constantly searching for greater power to see that in human affairs—especially at the highest level of political life, where not merely interests but vital principles of right and justice are at stake—the call for self-restraint is always destined to be a vain

---

*The fact that the Court had restrained itself with regard to national legislation for fifty years before handing down its decision in Dred Scott may well have helped to promote the acceptance of judicial power in some quarters. Seen from this perspective, the principle of restraint can often work as an ally of the cause of judicial supremacy, for it makes judicial revisions, when they occur, even more impressive. See Robert K. Faulkner, "Bickel's Constitution: The Problem of Moderate Liberalism," *American Political Science Review* 72 (September 1978): 925–40.

It is instructive that Lincoln never responded to the disastrous Dred Scott case with calls for greater restraint. "It is a duty, from which they may not shrink," Lincoln said of the Court in his First Inaugural Address, "to decide cases properly brought before them" (Collected Works, 4:268). Moreover, the argument that a body that had overturned an act of Congress only twice in its nearly seventy-year history should restrain itself would have surely sounded hollow.

request. The vigorous demand for self-restraint in scholarly literature, in judicial opinions, and in careful judicial selection—a line from James Thayer through Justices Felix Frankfurter and John Marshall Harlan to Alexander Bickel to Presidents Richard Nixon and Gerald Ford—seems to have had minimal effect. The Burger Court, even more than the Warren Court, is the surest proof of this opinion.*

The Founders did not establish the various departments of power with the expectation that political officials would—or should—restrain *themselves*. Consider the section of Justice Stone's observation that I quoted before: "the only check upon our own exercise of power is our own sense of self-restraint." Such a notion would strike the Founders as compelling evidence that a radical disjunction had taken place in the institutional development of the polity they created. As we have already seen, not self-restraint, not personal or institutional modesty, but interdepartmental checks lay at the core of the Founders' understanding. "The dignity and stability of government in all its branches," Jefferson declared in 1776, "depend so much upon an upright and skillful administration of justice, that the judicial power ought to be distinct from both the legislative and executive, and independent upon both so that it may be a check upon both, *as both should be checks upon that.*"[21] To the Founders, the security of both liberty and democracy rested first on the separation and independence of each branch, and then on that mutual activity of watching and checking.†

*Since Warren Burger has become chief justice, the Court has voided federal legislation in over three dozen instances, nullified more acts of Congress on First Amendment grounds than all of its predecessors combined, unanimously overruled the president on warrantless electronic surveillance, curtailed his activity on such political issues as executive privilege and impoundment, declared for the first time that busing may be used to overcome segregation in schools, greatly expanded the protection against gender-related discrimination, upset the various state procedures on the death penalty, and voided scores of state antiabortion statutes.

†In *Federalist* no. 10 Madison discusses the difficulties involved in any reliance on the self-restraint of ordinary mortals. The love of power and of fame,

The animating genius of the Founders' vision was the idea that each and every institution could be freed—allowed, in fact, to be active—because the activity of each branch could, within the internal structure of power, be watched, balanced, and checked. To grant great powers and then to expect the holders of those powers to exercise restraint would have appeared to the Founders as utopian, useless, and dangerous. Without the effective interaction and practical oversight of other branches, and the ultimate oversight of the popular vote, all the requirements of constitutional government would become "parchment barriers."[22] Surely this is more, not less, true when the department proclaiming the independent finality of its actions is effectively beyond direct popular control. And while it may be admitted that the historical erosion of the idea of reciprocal political checks on the Court has made judicial restraint more attractive, it is also true that the weakness of self-restraint should impel us to reconsider the importance of external checks.

Interdepartmental Checks and Judicial Power

It should be clear from the analysis so far that the problem of judicial power does not revolve around whether the Court should or should not have the power of judicial review. Rather, the important dispute is over the proper limits of judicial review. Nor does this investigation deny the propriety of the judicial independence that all free countries in the West have long cher-

---

partiality to one's own interests, and devotion to one's own opinions are wholly natural human passions. Consistent self-restraint simply demands too much of human nature. It is part of the argument of the *Federalist* papers that the solution to the social problem of self-interest could best be found in the liberation of human passions and desires and the external checking, in a diverse society, of their power to oppress others. This liberation and balancing of opinions and desires is developed in the fifty-first *Federalist*'s discussion of the internal checks implanted in the institutional structure of the government itself. See pp. 56–65 and 347–53.

ished. It merely seeks to remind us that judicial independence, like executive and congressional independence, necessarily exists within a total system of checks and balances in a constitutional democracy, within a system of designed redundancy wherein no one is sovereign save the people who ordained and established all three branches of political power. So the question is how to preserve a nation in which the principles of democratic rule, constitutionalism, and judicial review flourish and work and in which none is lost or diminished.

As we noted above, the principle of judicial finality—the principle that constitutional decisions of the Court are authoritative declarations of the meaning of the Constitution, subject to change only by amendment or judicial reversal—has been a major ingredient in the growth of judicial power and the erosion of the principles of popular sovereignty, constitutionalism, and interdepartmental checks. This analysis must now concentrate on the doctrine of finality, and not the general principle of the power of judicial review, for it is there, in the reputed final authority of an independent Court to tell the nation what its constitution demands it do and not do, that the whole issue of judicial supremacy is joined. The only reason the power of judges to rule imperially is even possible is that they find themselves in the position of authoritative interpreters of the constitutional text. At issue is not their right so to interpret. At issue, rather, is the context within which such a power exists and the proper restraints on the exercise of that power. So it is here, on the question of finality, on the question of judicial supremacy over the ultimate meaning of the constitutional text, that we should begin to reassess American judicial power.

Chapter 4 gave one instructive example of the ambiguity—the nonfinality, if we may call it that—of Supreme Court decisions: Jackson's action in the bank veto. Despite a clear and tightly reasoned decision written by the chief justice and supported without dissent by every other member of the Court upholding the constitutionality of the United States Bank,[23] Jackson vetoed a subsequent law renewing the bank's charter on openly constitutional grounds. "The opinion of the judges has no more authority over Congress than the opinion of the Congress have over the judges, and on that point the President is independent of both." "Each public official," Jackson's argument went, "who takes an oath to support the Constitution swears that he will support it as he understands it, and not as it is understood by others."[24]

History supports Jackson's analysis, at least to a point. No one argues that Congress must pass bills it fears are unconstitutional or that the president must sign them merely because the Court has previously held similar acts to be constitutionally proper. We hardly say that the Congress can refuse to act only when it holds proposals to be unwise or unnecessary or that the president can use his veto only when he thinks a bill unenforceable. In the process of legislation both the legislative and executive branches may declare that, in their views, an act is unconstitutional despite a Court ruling to the contrary. Despite the *ipse dixit* in *Cooper* v. *Aaron*, it is simply not true that the Court is "supreme in the exposition of the law of the Constitution" and that every interpretation of the Constitution by a Court majority is in and of itself the supreme law of the land. Congress and the president can act and have acted directly contrary to the Court's constitutional opinion, and have done so with absolute propriety. To repeat what was said in Chapter 4, if the Court is the final interpreter of our Constitution, it is final in a very ambiguous way.

This power of the political branches to decide unconstitutionality in opposition to the Court does not, in the public mind, seem to extend to the reverse, namely, the effective declaration of constitutionality in the face of the Court's contrary declaration. That is, it seems that Congress can effectively reverse a judicial opinion when the Court decides in favor of an action—that Congress can in those cases say the Court was wrong about the Constitution—but cannot do so when the Court decides against the action.*

*The new and growing power of courts to force legislative bodies to pass legislation—usually by requiring money to be appropriated or positions to be

It is central to the argument of this book that such a position is both philosophically and practically wrong: there *are* actions the political branches can take in the face of a negative constitutional ruling by the Court when a substantial segment of the people feel such a decision to be unwise, unjust, or erroneous. There are actions that the people, acting through their representatives, can take to reverse a ruling by the judiciary and to make the process of constitutional adjudication and interpretation a shared endeavor of the polity as a whole, and not the final prerogative of the Court. Such actions are not constitutional, historical, or logical oddities. Rather, they are legitimate and reasonable means by which, in a system of checks and balances, the power of judicial review can be kept from devolving into the practice of judicial finality. My aim up to this point has been to elucidate the theory on which there can develop those practices that treat the Court as a coequal and contributing branch of government, checked as well as checking, independent but not absolute.

We should begin by admitting the obvious—that checking a court bent on actively directing the course of legislation and the policy of the nation is never easy. To be sure, some evident checks on the power of the Court are written into the body of the Constitution itself, checks every student learns in basic American government classes: impeachment, the power of Congress to regulate and make exceptions to the appellate jurisdiction of the Court, and "court-packing."[25] The fact is, of course,

---

created—will, if it continues, soon bring us to the point where the above analysis is no longer correct. Courts may soon wield the power of vesting constitutional rights and then demand that Congress and the state legislatures support the exercise of those rights, even though Congress and the states may doubt their legitimacy. The recent attempt in the lower courts to have Congress fund abortions is a clear case in point. To the extent that this tendency becomes settled fact—the more judges can set policies, force appropriations for them, and demand or oversee their execution—"the accumulation of all powers: legislative, executive and judicial" are truly in the same hands. And such unchecked power is exactly what Madison did not hesitate to call "the very definition of tyranny" (*Federalist*, no. 47, p. 324).

that these rather obvious constitutional checks on judicial power are extremely severe, politically impossible, or both.

Consider impeachment. Hamilton shocks us in *Federalist* 81 when, in response to antifederalist fears of judicial supremacy, he rather cavalierly states that if particular justices engage in "deliberate usurpations on the authority of the legislature," the simple solution is impeachment. "This alone," he declares, "is a complete security."[26] But impeachment not only verges on the politically impossible, as Jefferson soon found out when he tried it against the Federalist-dominated judiciary; it also, in a liberal society, has awkward moral-philosophical implications. In fact, the reason impeachment is impossible politically is in large measure that it seems extremely inappropriate morally. Impeachment of sitting justices for criminal activity or manifest incompetence is surely supportable. But impeachment to remedy judicial decisions smacks too much of a punishment imposed for the expression of an opinion, for the exercise of a duty laid upon one by force of oath and office, for the statement of a thoughtful judgment. Again, the problem is not in the Founders' intention—they intended, as Hamilton makes evident, to have clear reciprocal checks on judicial power. They had no desire to allow simple beliefs in judicial independence or judicial finality to undercut the principle of mutual checks and balances. The problem was in the lack of sufficient care, attributable perhaps to their contention of judicial weakness, in fashioning these reciprocal checks. In any event, this "complete security" that Hamilton described was later better characterized by Jefferson, who called it "a scarecrow."[27]*

The Constitution also says that the Court exercises its appellate jurisdiction (that is, almost all it does) "with such Exceptions, and under such Regulations as the Congress shall make."[28] Thus Congress can remove—and legitimately has removed—

---

*Jefferson also labeled Congress' impeachment power over the judiciary "nugatory," "inefficient," and "a farce" (*Writings of Thomas Jefferson*, 15:21, 16:114, 9:191).

the Court's ability to hear certain cases by denying it jurisdiction in particular instances.* Edward S. Corwin in fact cites this grant of "unlimited control" over the Court's appellate jurisdiction, along with its equally "unlimited" power over the size of the Court, as "the chief external restraint upon judicial review."[29]

The truth is, however, that this restraint on the exercise of wayward judicial power, like impeachment, has serious political liabilities, not the least of which is that it seems to demand that considerations of the constitutional legitimacy of particular legislative acts be, a priori, closed in certain areas. Thus, in the very exercise of a power granted with seeming constitutional clarity, Congress finds itself verging on the very type of autonomous legislative activity that the principle of constitutionalism was meant to deflect.

Moreover, the ability of Congress to use this clause as an effective check on judicial power is currently undergoing major reconsideration. The common and once universal opinion was that spoken by Chief Justice Salmon P. Chase in *McCardle*: "We are not at liberty to inquire into the motives of the Legislature. We can only examine into its power under the Constitution; and the power to make exceptions to the appellate jurisdiction of this court is given by express words."[30] Or, as Justice Samuel Chase put it in 1799, "the disposal of the judicial power ... belongs to Congress."[31] But recent scholarship has brought these broad formulations under increasingly strenuous attack. Some commentators deny Congress the ability to use its power to "negate the essential functions of the Supreme Court."[32] Others deny Congress the power to act if it should seek to remove all or even a major part of the Court's appellate jurisdiction.[33] Still others would void all congressional attempts to use its power

---

*The Habeas Corpus Act of March 27, 1868, upheld in *Ex parte McCardle*, 7 Wallace 506 (1869), is the leading instance of congressional action under this power. It is by no means the only time Congress has so acted. During the New Deal, for example, Congress restricted the power of federal courts to issue labor injunctions. See the Norris-LaGuardia Act, chap. 90, 47 Stat. 70 (1932); 29 U.S.C. §101–15 (1976).

over appellate jurisdiction to deny rights that could not otherwise be denied.[34]

That Congress has *some* usable power over the Court under
the exceptions clause is undeniable. The constitutional text is
comparatively unambiguous, the precedents are solid, the Court
has been overwhelmingly favorable to a broad approach to
congressional power in this area, and, finally, the arguments
that try to destroy all congressional authority often sound thin
and tendentious.* Still, it must be admitted that the full scope
of Congress' power in this area is no longer completely clear.

The last of the textbook restraints on the Court—Congress'
ability to alter the size of the Court—has perhaps fewer theoretical obstacles before it, though it surely has many formidable
political difficulties. Congress changed the size of the Court (for
reasons that clearly included the wish to reverse its decisions or
affect its interpretive drift) with fair regularity throughout the
first half of the nineteenth century. But the tactic has not been
used in well over a century and its failure in the Court-packing
fight of 1937 probably signaled the permanent defeat of this
stratagem as a method of checking judicial policy.†

---

*The legal attack on any congressional power under the exceptions clause
is more rhetorical than persuasive. Lawrence Gene Sager, for example, calls
the possibility of such congressional action "an assault," "dangerous," and "taw-
dry" ("Constitutional Limitations on Congress' Authority to Regulate the Jurisdiction of the Federal Courts," *Harvard Law Review* 95 [November 1981]:89).
Note how odd it is that many of the loudest defenders of untrammeled judicial
power are hesitant to let the Court decide in these instances what, in the Court's
own view, the proper limits or extent of congressional power really may be.
If, as we have heard it argued, it is the Court that defines for us the Constitution,
we should welcome congressional action in this area and move the debate out
of the law journals and into the courts. One gets the sense that the arguments
against congressional activity in this area are so loud simply in order to prevent
the Court from considering the issue, since the Court may well side with Congress on the matter.

†The clearest case of this nature was also the last, in 1869. However, Alfred
H. Kelly and Winfred A. Harbison (*The American Constitution*, 5th ed. [New
York: Norton, 1976], pp. 453–54) dispute the notion that this tactic was used
to change the decision in Hepburn v. Griswold (75 U.S. 603). If their view is
correct, it then becomes questionable whether court-packing to reverse a Court's

Lacking the ability to pack the Court, presidents still have the power, subject to the advice and consent of the Senate, to appoint new justices as vacancies arise. This has been a somewhat effective method of directing the course of the judiciary over time, but the opportunity to make an occasional appointment is hardly an efficacious way of responding to a particular decision or set of decisions. (Franklin Roosevelt, for example, had to wait until 1937 to name his first appointee.) It depends on death or resignation—and, moreover, the death or resignation of the "appropriate" justices.

The power of appointment is also hardly a very precise check on judicial activity. Jefferson's (and Madison's) ill luck with nominees to the bench is still instructive. Lincoln had similar difficulties. Woodrow Wilson's first appointee was James McReynolds; neither Calvin Coolidge nor Warren Harding could have been fully content with Harlan Stone or Benjamin Cardozo. Dwight Eisenhower's dissatisfaction with Earl Warren and William Brennan is well known; and, except perhaps for Warren Burger and William Rehnquist, the Nixon-Ford nominees will forever chagrin those who appointed them. The conclusion is that to approach an unwarranted *decision* by waiting for a good vacancy is to leave the matter simply to chance.

There are, to be sure, other checks—less formal and often self-generated checks—on judicial activity, but they do not, by themselves, rise to the level of formidable restraints on the Court's activity. Some of these checks—respect for precedent, the doctrine of "political questions," principles of standing, ripeness, and mootness—are checks only in the loosest sense possible, being largely fashioned and fashionable at judicial will. The effective decline of even these restraints (and, with them, the

---

direction has ever been used in American history, although both packing and unpacking have surely been used to *preserve* a particular judicial direction. (Consider the attempt of the Federalists to deprive the Jeffersonians of an appointment by reducing the number of seats from six to five in 1801 and the strengthening of Jacksonianism by the increase from seven to nine in 1837).

persuasiveness of the arguments for judicial self-restraint) points out even more sharply the independence verging on autonomy of the modern Court. Other informal, nonconstitutional restraints—the power of the clerks, the foot-dragging of lower courts, the criticisms of professors in law reviews and professional journals—are simply, by themselves, insufficient. No one would be swayed to release the presidency from the restraints placed on it—from a limited term of office and the necessity of reelection, for example—by the argument that all presidents read the papers, are stung by criticism, and fear the verdict of impartial history. Clearly, neither self-generated nor informal checks are enough, by themselves, to satisfy the demands of constitutional government.

On the other side, we should be very reluctant to fashion for the Court the same checks that work in other areas of American politics. This analysis is not, for example, a covert argument for rotation in the judicial office, regularization of judicial recall, or the periodic election of federal judges. True, such projects are not outrageous or unthinkable. And, in a nation without any effective restraint on the power of judges, such solutions may even rise to the level of necessity. But we hardly have reason to consider checks beyond our present constitutional structure without first weighing all the possibilities actually still available.

The various textbook checks on the Court—impeachment, removal of jurisdiction, and modifications of the Court's size—though generally unusable, do point to the fact that the constitutional independence allowed the judicial branch was, like executive independence, to be understood as existing within a whole framework of constitutional—that is, limited—government.* But impeachment, denial of jurisdiction, and court-pack-

*The existence of these powers over the Court in the hands of the elected branches points directly to the fact that the Court was not considered so independent as to be beyond the oversight and power of Congress and the executive. The oddest objection to this view is the position once put forward by Raoul Berger. Berger argues that the impeachment, court packing, and exceptions powers cannot be constitutional ways of checking the Court because the Constitution would not confer the power of judicial review with one hand and threaten its limitation with the other. Both to grant a power and to give

ing are, in effect, incommensurate with the problem. They are too heavy or too blunt a set of instruments to use against the Court. All such powers do more than give the democracy revisionary power over unwarranted decisions. All are more or less severe attacks on the Court's ability to function as an institution. In most cases it is a decision, not the general powers or personnel of the Court, that requires a rejoinder from the other branches of government. To attack the powers of the judiciary or the personnel of the Court in order to reach and reverse a particular decision is excessive, generally unwarranted, and almost always indefensible. Partly because these obvious checks on the Court are so strikingly incommensurate with the problem at hand, the judiciary has found it relatively easy to augment its constitutional hegemony.

So the question necessarily recurs: In a nation that seeks to make effective the necessary balance between judicial power and democratic will, what checks are left on the Court, on judicial decisions, equivalent to the Court's check on the powers of the democracy?

Effective Checks on Judicial Supremacy

"This Court," Justice Frankfurter once noted, "may be asked to reconsider its decisions, and this has been done successfully

---

the means of limiting its exercise seems to Berger akin to the Founders' "chasing their tails around a stump" (*Congress v. the Supreme Court*, p. 357; see also all of chap. 9, pp. 285–97, especially pp. 293–94). But this position mistakes the very essence of checks and balances—that the branches were meant, literally, to check each other.

William Crosskey, on the other side, finds the potential power of the elected branches over the Court so obvious that he refuses to believe that the Founders could have intended the Court to have judicial review. Such a situation would mean that the Founders were "incredibly careless," giving with one hand what they left potentially restricted with the other (*Politics and the Constitution*, 2:981).

Clearly, to both absolutist positions, checks and balances will always seem a contradition, for they do deny clean, final, and evident lines of sovereign power to any one branch of government. The framers designed a structure in which each branch has power and oversight over each of the others, and left the final sovereign authority in the hands of the people only.

again and again throughout our history."[35] In various forms and in various modes this power of Congress literally to force reconsideration in most areas of constitutional law is one of the least examined and least acknowledged methods that the political branches have to respond to judicial rulings.

Perhaps the most common form in which this dialogue between Congress and the Court has occurred and may continue to occur is under Congress' unquestioned ability to rewrite voided legislation in order to pass judicial scrutiny. Such action can, on the one hand, take the form of congressional enactment of the same legislation in alternate constitutional guise, as when Congress tried to ban the worst abuses of child labor first under its commerce power, then, after that approaches was rejected, under its taxing power, then once more (and successfully) under the commerce clause.[36] Similarly, the Court was led to distinguish (without, some might say, a difference) between religious instruction in the public schools (which was forbidden) and "released time" from school hours for exactly that purpose.[37] "The political branches," as Raoul Berger has written, "retain at all times the crucial ability to force the Court to reexamine in new context the validity of the constitutional position it has previously taken."[38]

The clearest examples of Congress' refusal to be bound by the Court's "final" determination of constitutionality are found in the area of civil rights. Despite major decisions of the Court to the contrary,[39] no one today doubts the power of Congress to protect the basic civil rights of minorities to speak, to assemble, to vote, and to be free from summary executions. Despite a near unanimous Court to the contrary,* no one considers it illegitimate for Congress to outlaw discrimination in transportation, housing, theaters, inns, or public places of amusement.[40] There is, in fact, hardly any major civil rights legislation today on the books that does not stand in open rejection of the Court's earlier

---

*The Civil Rights Cases, 109 U.S. 3 (1883), overturned the Civil Rights Act of 1875 and were the controlling cases on these matters until the 1960s.

considered judgment on the true and final meaning of the Constitution.

In the congressional debate over the framing of the Civil Rights Act of 1964, an act in which Congress bluntly rejected the holding in the *Civil Rights Cases* of 1883, Senator John Pastore put the issue succinctly and colorfully:

> I am a little disturbed about the carefulness we are exercising on both sides here with relation to the inviolability of an opinion of the Supreme Court of 1883. I submit that until it is changed by another opinion of the Supreme Court, or by constitutional amendment, that it is the binding law of the land and we must preserve it. But is there any constitutional prohibition about Congress taking a second bite at the cherry?
> Mr. [Burke] Marshall [assistant attorney general, Civil Rights Division]: No, there isn't, Senator.[41]

Whether through the ruse of working through the commerce clause or by discovering powers earlier hidden within the words of the Reconstruction Amendments,[42] Congress has managed to pass civil rights laws despite a host of important court decisions to the contrary. There seems to be nothing in either history or theory that forbids congressional attempts to revive acts the courts have overturned.

At times the legislative changes made to resuscitate a voided law are minimal—as in the second Agricultural Adjustment Act, which was in its "essential features and purposes" the same as the first AAA, which the Court upset in *United States* v. *Butler*.[43] The child labor law of 1938 was constitutionally indistinguishable from the law the Court voided in 1905. And there are instances when the Congress has simply repassed the offending statute, not seeking to have the Court distinguish but simply to have to relent.* "In short," as Corwin has pointed out, "while

---

*Rewriting aims at leading the Court to distinguish the new legislation from that which was rejected. Reenactment, as in the Territories Act of 1862 or in Congress' reinstatement of the right to collective bargaining in the Wagner Act after the Court voided the National Industrial Recovery Act in the Schechter case, aims simply at having the Court back down. See Bickel, *Least Dangerous Branch*, p. 263, in regard to the Guffey-Snyder Bituminous Coal Bill.

the Court can and must decide *cases* according to its own independent view of the Constitution, it does not in so doing fix the *Constitution* for an indefinite future."[44] Or, as Lincoln said in the face of *Dred Scott*: "Were I in Congress and a vote should come up on a question whether slavery should be prohibited in a new territory, in spite of that Dred Scott decision, I would vote that it should."[45] Congress, "in spite of that Dred Scott decision," debated and passed exactly such a bill in 1862, and Lincoln, as president, signed it.[46]

Lincoln indicated in 1857 the basis for this constitutional position of congressional interaction with judicial decisions. "We think," Lincoln said regarding the Court,

> its decisions on Constitutional questions, when fully settled, should control, not only the particular cases decided, but the general policy of the country, subject to be disturbed only by the amendments of the Constitution as provided in that instrument itself. More than this would be revolution. But we think the Dred Scott decision is erroneous. We know the Court that made it has often over-ruled its own decisions, and we shall do what we can to have it over-rule this.[47]

President Jackson had earlier set the grounds for such a response: "Each public officer who takes an oath to support the Constitution swears that he will support it as he understands it and not as it is understood by others."[48]* Although, as I have

*The only significant difference between Lincoln and Jackson on this matter is that Lincoln was more prepared to admit that in the end, the Court would have to be respected and accepted as interpretively superior to the other branches for the sake of preserving the security of constitutional government: "[If the question of slavery in the territories] had been before the court more than once, and had there been affirmed and re-affirmed through a course of years, it then might be, perhaps would be, factious, nay, even revolutionary, to not acquiesce" (speech at Springfield, June 26, 1857, in Lincoln, *Collected Works*, 2:40). To Jackson, on the other hand, even the longest string of judicial precedents was still not binding "except where the acquiescence of the people and the States can be considered as well settled" (Jackson, veto message of July 10, 1832, in *Messages and Papers*, ed. Richardson, 2:576).

This distinction is significant. America is grounded in tension between the ultimate rule of law, or constitutionalism, and the ultimate rule the people, popular sovereignty. This tension clouds the theoretical waters. Lincoln's unargued, this position cannot justifiably be stretched to give the executive the right to pick and choose what laws or decisions he will enforce, it does mean that the decision in a particular case need not become a principle that binds Congress and the president in their understanding of the Constitution or their understanding of what future enactments they may or may not pass. Again, the decision in a particular case at hand, the holding regarding the parties and the particular law in question, binds all branches as it does the litigants themselves. There can be no alternative if we mean to preserve the rule of law. But the particular holding need not necessarily bind further. Judicial interpretations do not settle for the political branches the permanent meaning of the Constitution's text or its principles. Such interpretations surely do not bind the Court, which retains the right to reverse itself in future cases. Nor, in like manner, does it necessarily bind future actions of the Congress or the president.* Although the decision in each case must necessarily stand, the opinion of the Court on the constitutional question before it, on the meaning of the Constitution itself, need not become, as Lincoln put it, a "rule of political action" for all the other branches.[49]† It is upon this fact that a practice of congressional interaction with the Court can be built.

---

derstanding was that, in the end, the orderly process of law must be the binding force, unless we intend to be "revolutionary"—that is, overthrow the established order. To Jackson the tension was best resolvable, in the end, by deference to democratic power. This means, in practice, that Jacksonians would have less hesitancy in using the powers of impeachment, denial of jurisdiction, and court-packing than would Lincoln, for those powers are effective means of asserting the power of the majority over the institutionalized process of law. Franklin Roosevelt's defense of his bill to "reorganize" the judiciary was derived, in that regard, more from Jackson's position than from Lincoln's. Significant as this distinction may be "in the end," it is relegated to the obscurity of a footnote because this book is concerned with the available powers and limits of the democratic response to judicial decrees not *in extremis* but before then.

*"A legislature without exceeding its province cannot reverse a determination once made; though it may prescribe a new rule for future cases" *(Federalist,* no. 81, p. 545).

†Although congressional reversals of Supreme Court decisions in the area of civil rights are the most spectacular, even the most pedestrian examples are

The power of Congress repeatedly to call for reexamination and reconsideration of the Court's "final" interpretations obviously lacks the immediate strength, let us say, of the power of Congress to override a presidential veto. Yet history has supported its general effectiveness, especially when it is buttressed by timely presidential appointments or sympathetic legal scholarship, and constitutional theory fully supports its use, indeed, its increased use.

In addition to repeating its attempts to secure judicial acceptance of a statute by either rewriting or repassing it, Congress also has the ability to circumscribe the holding of any decision in an attempt to delimit its effects. The most obvious example of congressional attempts to minimize the impact of a particular decisions is the body of legislation that was passed in response to the Court's abortion decrees.[50] Congress had forbidden Medicaid payments for certain types of abortions, banned the use of funds for abortions as a method of family planning under the Foreign Assistance Act, banned fetal research, prohibited Legal Service attorneys from handling abortion-related cases, and passed a "conscience clause" amendment to the Hill-Burton Act indicating Congress' continuing financial support for any hospital, public or private, which refuses on the basis of religious or moral belief to perform abortions.[51] Many of these acts will come before the Court, and there they may be overturned. But

---

instructive. In 1929 the Court declared that the Court of Custom Appeals was not a court within the meaning of Art. III of the Constitution (Ex parte Bakelite Corp., 279 U.S. 439; see also Williams v. United States, 289 U.S. 553 [1933]). In Glidden v. Zdanak, 370 U.S. 530 (1962), however, the Court deferred to Congress' determination that the courts of custom appeals "were created under Article III." The McCarren Act, which conferred on the states the power to regulate insurance companies doing business in interstate commerce, flew directly in the face of Cooley v. Board of Wardens, 12 Howard 299 (1851). When confronted with this congressional rejection of a major and historic Supreme Court ruling, the Court unanimously sustained Congress (Prudential v. Benjamin, 328 U.S. 408 [1946]. If, as we are often told, the Court is not exempt from heeding the will of the people, one way to help the people prevail is for Congress simply to act.

that fact in no way derogates from Congress' constitutional ability, as an equal and independent branch of government, to enter
into this type of constitutional dialogue with the Court, through
legislation, on matters of vital national concern. The more important the issue, in fact, the more necessary the dialogue. And
here is exactly where the various informal restraints on the
Court—the pressure of democratic opinion, the arguments in
leading journals, and the president's power to fill vacancies with
carefully selected new members, for example—can have increased effectiveness. On important constitutional questions involving important aspects of national life and policy, the setting
of constitutional doctrine is not to be left, with simply finality,
to the Court.

Oddly enough, considering all the varieties of public checks
on judicial power, the relatively easy legislative responses mentioned here may be among the most effective. The writing of a
rejected statute in revised form or on a different constitutional
base (or even the reenactment of the same law under similar
terms)[52] and the discovery of ways beyond constitutional sus-
picion to limit the impact of a particular judicial holding both
have a decent history of success—far more success, that is, than
the use of the amending power, court-packing, impeachment,
or limiting the Court's appellate jurisdiction.[53] These congressional challenges to judicial decisions and interpretations also
have, as we noted before, the advantage of focusing attention
not on the merits of judicial review itself, or on the personnel
of the Court, but exactly where the public dialogue belongs, on
the decision in controversy, on the constitutional question itself.

Beyond the introduction of new legislation that argues for
a differing constitutional view, there may be more speculative
and tentative means of framing congressional responses to judicial acts. One avenue of approach has even been suggested
by the Court itself: in speaking of the Fourteenth Amendment,
Justice Brennan once noted, "The primary purpose of the
Amendment was to augment the power of Congress, not the
judiciary."[54] But Congress' full powers under that amendment—

under, for example, the long-neglected privileges and immunities clause—have rarely been examined or tested. In the abortion controversy, to take one example, the rights of fetuses may well find protection within the broad reach of this section. Given the fact that the Reconstruction Amendments were written to sweep away the last vestige of history's most blatant case of judicial overextension, it is difficult to believe that the Court alone is the ultimate decider of the meaning of constitutional liberty under those amendments. Those amendments vested in Congress—not in the Court, not in the states—the overriding authority to define, delineate, and defend the civil rights of all Americans.

Moreover, under the fifth section of the Fourteenth Amendment, Congress is given "the power to enforce by appropriate legislation the provisions of this article." "The manner of enforcement involves discretion," Justice William O. Douglas once noted, "but that discretion is largely entrusted to Congress, not the Courts."[55] If the interpretation and enforcement of the great and inclusive rights embraced by the Fourteenth Amendment were as firmly in congressional hands as they now are in judicial hands—if Congress exercised its power "to define the substantive scope of the Amendment" as well as "the manner of enforcement"[56]—that vital continuing dialectic between judicial insight and democratic needs and desires would soon become a constitutional reality.* It may well be that here, in the expan-

---

*For the most restrictive view of congressional power, see the Civil Rights Cases, 109 U.S. 3 (1883). For a more open view, see Katzenbach v. Morgan, 384 U.S. 641 (1966), 668. The discussion in the latter case is somewhat muddied by Brennan's remark that "Congress' power under sec. 5 is limited to adopting measures to enforce the guarantees of the Amendment. Sec. 5 grants Congress no power to restrict, abrogate or dilute those guarantees" (651n10). Yet while surely Congress may not enforce the amendment by abrogating its guarantees, it is not clear that Congress is forbidden to define the full range of privileges and rights differently than the Court or to restrict, abrogate, or dilute the remedies *of the Court* (see Harlan's dissent at 668).

This latter point is helped along by the recent case of Fullilove v. Klutznick, 448 U.S. 448 (1980), upholding the right of the government to earmark at least 10 percent of federal funds granted for local public works projects to businesses owned by minority group members. Recognizing that sec. 5 of the Fourteenth Amendment does not "render [congressional enactments] immune

sive powers purposely vested in Congress under the Fourteenth Amendment, the best response to all instances of judicial over-extension may finally be found.

These few practical solutions may seem exceedingly modest and minimal. What took pages of history and philosophy to prepare us for has here been described in a few short para-graphs—paragraphs, in fact, that tell us what to avoid about as strongly as they recommend to us a course of action. I realize the brevity of these solutions while at the same time I recognize the fact that at present there are probably no others. Yet I also recognize the potential efficacy of these solutions. Though briefly stated, they can, if applied, have wide-ranging repercussions. Our full understanding of the extent of congressional power under section 5 of the Fourteenth Amendment, for example, is only now starting to be worked out. If Congress takes that path, or other paths mentioned above, someday volumes will be written.

I have put aside any argument for the most extreme checks on the judiciary, such as impeachment and court-packing. I have also left unpursued what might be described as a more proce-dural method by which Congress may govern the courts, as by defining minimum standards for standing or by establishing narrower requirements for class action suits. All such attempts to restrain judicial activism through the establishment of pro-cedural fences around the courts have substantial merit and

---

from judicial scrutiny," the Court nevertheless reasserted the argument in Katzenbach v. Morgan, equating the scope of sec. 5 with the scope of Congress' power under the commerce clause and the necessary and proper clause. The Court, in fact, suggested that sec. 5 may be conceived of as broader than the grant under the commerce clause: "In certain contexts, there are limitations on the reach of the Commerce Power to regulate the actions of state and local governments. *National League of Cities v. Usery* 426 U.S. 833 (1976). To avoid such complications, we look to sec. 5 of the Fourteenth Amendment.... " In this regard congressional power under sec. 5, although reviewable by the Court, is also far broader than the power of the Court: "Congress, of course, may legislate without compiling the kind of 'record' [here, regarding evidence of prior discrimination] appropriate with respect to judicial or administrative pro-ceedings.... It is beyond question, therefore, that Congress has the authority to identify unlawful discriminatory practices, to prohibit those practices, and to prescribe remedies to eradicate their continuing effects."

deserve serious legal consideration.[57] I have, however, avoided siding fully with this tactic for three reasons. First, although reducing the opportunity for courts to do mischief will no doubt reduce mischief, it is only a partial answer; we still need to know what to do when courts go over or around the procedural fence. Would such remedies have prevented *Roe* v. *Wade?* Second, I wished to reach the truly burning issue of contemporary judicial politics, namely, the degree to which Congress can respond to particular *decisions* of the Court that Congress finds intolerable or unconstitutional. Third, I am not yet certain that we should want a Court so bound that, while it may decide "concrete cases," it is prevented from "pondering abstract principles."[58] In ways that will seem treasonous to many readers who have supported this book's argument so far, the final chapter will describe why a Court that is both checked and active may well be the optimal constitutional solution. Judicial supremacy is constitutionally intolerable; but strict judicial quiescence is a constitutional mistake.

In many ways the perfect constitutional solution to the problem of interpretive finality and judicial imperialism would have been for the judiciary to possess the same legislative relationship to Congress as that which governs the executive. Just as Congress, by special majority, can override a presidential veto, a similar process could from the outset have been established to review judicial objections. To have subjected judicial "vetoes" to the same process of review as that to which the Constitution subjects presidential vetoes would have been the most unobjectionable method of combining the benefit of active judicial reasoning and scrutiny with final democratic oversight. It would have been the perfect balancing of the principle of constitutionalism with active popular sovereignty.

Such a process is exactly what Madison had in mind when he proposed the idea of "requiring bills to be separately communicated to the Executive and Judicial departments. If either of these object, let two-thirds, if both, three fourths, of each House be necessary to overrule the objection." Such a plan would have preserved all the benefits of review "without disarming the Legislature of its requisite authority."[59] If overruled, neither the

Court nor the president could then have treated the law as unconstitutional or invalid.*

In this regard it is worth pointing out that even Chief Justice Marshall was willing to consider favorably the propriety of formal congressional reversals of Court decisions. Jefferson's "doctrine" of impeachment, Marshall wrote to Samuel Chase in 1804, "should yield to an appellate jurisdiction in the legislature. A reversal of those legal opinions deemed unsound by the legislature would certainly better comport with the mildness of our character than a removal of the judge who has rendered them unknowing of his fault."[60]

The aim of this book, however, is to lay out the theoretical framework that will support scholars and statesmen as they think through the currently available means by which Congress can respond to judicial acts. Though the benefits of having had a regular procedure for considering judicial reversals as we have for presidential vetoes would have been of significant benefit to America, we would do best to put off considering efforts in that direction until all the present means of congressional oversight have been exhausted.†

---

*The idea of relying on a joint "Council of Revision" came up a number of times at the Constitutional Convention. (See Farrand, ed., *Records of the Federal Convention*, 1:21, 97–98, 108; 2:73, 75, 78, 298, 300.) All versions of the idea were variations on the Madison plan. The proposals failed partly because of the innocent hope that the Court could be "kept out of politics" and partly because of erroneous fears that such a mechanism might give the Court a double veto—first in conjunction with the president, then, if Congress overrode that veto, on its own account. Such a fear was certainly ill founded, since (as Madison knew) "a qualified negative on legislative *bills* would have precluded the question of a Judiciary amendment of Legislative *Acts*" (Madison to Monroe, December 27, 1819, in *Writings of James Madison*, 8:406).

†To subject judicial decisions to a formal procedure for congressional oversight and review, as in the case of presidential vetoes, would today surely require a constitutional amendment. Enough constitutional history has passed without such a formal procedure to make its establishment a substantial departure from ordinary political practice. Lacking explicit procedures for the exercise of judicial review in the text of the Constitution, however, it may have been wholly appropriate for Congress, early in our history, in setting out the modes of and procedures governing the exercise of judicial power, to have then, by statute, set up formal procedures of judicial-congressional interaction.

The various methods of congressional response that have been touched on in this chapter all fall far short of the more obvious, but also more futile, checks of impeachment, removal of jurisdiction, and packing the Court. Needless to say, the direction indicated in this analysis is more modest. Needless also to say, it is a direction, not a program, not a formula for particular action. In that task, the work of many hands is needed. But without further work, future constitutional history will all too closely resemble the past, fluctuating between simplistic sentiments of judicial supremacy and more or less impetuous attempts to "curb" the Court, with the Court all the while increasing its progressive hegemony over public and private life.

No doubt a practical objection will be raised to this approach: though it may have both the power and the means, Congress hardly has the desire to withstand the directive powers of the courts. Insofar as members of Congress have been able to extricate themselves from hard decisions, decisions especially about constitutionality, they have done so, and they may continue to do so. The judiciary, the presidency, and the bureaucracy have all increased their effectiveness because, in the exercise of power, Congress has substantially abdicated its independent responsibility to consider, interpret, and apply, by its own lights, the demands of the constitutional text. The contemporary fact is

---

The Judiciary Act of 1789, wherein Congress (in sec. 25) legislatively recognized the right of judicial review (substantially before the Marbury case was decided), would have been the obvious place to do so. Having delineated the power of judicial review, unmentioned in the text of the Constitution, Congress could also have delineated particular modes of its activity. Moreover, this right of final legislative oversight patterned on presidential-congressional interaction could have been claimed from the nature of the legislative function (similar to Marshall's derivation of review from the nature of the judicial function), buttressed, perhaps, by the constitutional injunction (Art. III, sec. 2) that Congress "regulate" the appellate jurisidiction of the judicial system, and by Congress' power to make all laws "necessary and proper" to put into execution "the power vested by this Constitution in the government of the United States, or in any department or office thereof" (Art. I, sec. 8).

that judicial activism is always more probable than congressional activism.

The degree to which that objection is true is the degree to which the problem of judicial imperialism will be irremediable. If or when Congress does abdicate, and either swallow its objections to the activity of others or encourage others to act as substitutes for itself, then checks and balances will become a factual impossibility. Still, as the power of judges to legislate actively grows—the power, for example, to appropriate funds for various social welfare programs—the need for congressional—that is, public—responses will grow increasingly greater. Nevertheless, this book cannot hope to prod Congress to act. It can only elucidate the principles on which Congress may act if and when it finds the erosion of its powers intolerable or a particular decision unsupportable. All that can now be done is to lay out those principles that will help to prevent our attachment to the rule of law from becoming a belief in the rule of judges, and hope that the principles will find effective life as they are needed. Or to turn the answer around, our other hope is that, if a reaction to judicial supremacy ultimately does occur, it will not be carried out against the principle of judicial review or against the Court as an institution, but rather will take the form of restoring the Court to its proper place in a system of checked and balanced powers.

The greater the recognition that the Court's interpretations of the Constitution need not be immediately accepted as binding "rules of political action"—the greater the acknowledgment that the process of constitutional definition is a process shared among the branches and with the people—the more sanguine may be our future hopes of recapturing in practice that constitutional balance we have so far reviewed in theory. If the basic outlines of this rather philosophic inquiry are true, what is now needed is for legal scholars and public figures to increase and develop the means whereby the dialogue between Court and nation can more properly take place. Further inquiry into appropriate political ways of checking judicial decisions is still obviously necessary, for there is no doubt that the theory here elucidated of a partnership rather than a hierarchy in the shaping of constitutional government is easier described in principle than developed into actions. In sum, what is still needed is for scholars, politicians, and jurists to direct their attentions to the means whereby the Court can take its proper place in a nation dedicated to democratic governance under the rule of a permanent and principled Constitution.

6 *The Promise and*
Perils of an Active Court

Courts have certain capacities for dealing with matters
of principle that legislatures and executives do not
possess.

—ALEXANDER BICKEL

The formative document of American political life, the Declaration of Independence, describes in sharp and ringing words
the essential meaning of this republic. "We hold these truths to
be self-evident, that all men are created equal, that they are
endowed by their Creator with certain unalienable rights, that
among these are life, liberty and the pursuit of happiness. That
to secure these rights, governments are instituted among men,
deriving their just powers from the consent of the governed."
The American vision, a vision we thought worthy of promulgating to all the "candid world," was exactly that promise of
equal liberty. The promise has not always been kept; at times it
has come near to being renounced. Yet without the continued
effort to secure and perfect the right to equal liberty, no American government can claim for itself respect or legitimacy.

The end of government is, then, the security and enjoyment

of certain natural rights, some of which the Declaration calls out by name. But, beyond that end, we are a nation dedicated to a particular political means, to a government based on what the Declaration calls "the consent of the governed." We have, as a nation, committed ourselves to something more than the protection of liberty. We have decided to secure our liberty in what some may fear is the most difficult and tenuous way: we have decided to secure freedom under the form and substance of democratic government. Both liberty and democracy are the necessary hallmarks of legitimate American politics.

In consciously attempting to blend, perhaps for the first time in human history, individual liberty with democratic government, the Founders of this nation were quite properly cautious. Political power, the historic nemesis of private right, was to be severely circumscribed, watched, and checked. The full force of democratic rule would be muted, tempered by a written constitution, by a large and diverse territory, by staggered terms of office, by a variety of methods and modes of election, by bicameralism, separation of powers, checks and balances. Yet, having taken all the necessary precautions toward the elimination of the particular diseases of democratic government, the public as a whole was still to be the ruling element, not the power of any individual, class, clique, or institution. America was dedicated to the difficult task of securing the blessings of liberty for all in a nation ruled not by the simply wise or just but by the people, by both "the spirit and form of popular government," by what Hamilton called "the deliberate sense of the community."[1]

Within that context let us consider the Court. The only possible defense of an institution of life-tenured, nonelected jurists with substantial power over vital aspects of political life and private conduct is that such a body has the potential to help us attain what we in this society permanently desire, the enunciation and realization of those principles that have made our life together as a nation distinctive and praiseworthy, and to do it with sufficient regard for the demands of democratic rule. The principles of equal liberty, enunciated by the Declaration of

Independence and formulated into politics by the Constitution, may well be self-evident, but they are hardly self-executing. They require application, dedication, and understanding. Only insofar as the Court can encourage the democracy to preserve, protect, and promote its own high principles can we fully justify its great power to share in our rule. In other words, the principle of equal liberty and the principle of representative democracy together show us both the basis of judicial power and the boundaries that circumscribe its exercise.

Separation of Powers and the Protection of Equal Liberty

The classic defense of judicial power always embodied the idea, or the hope, that the Court would help the democracy preserve its constitutional heritage intact, its self-evident but difficult aspirations. More particularly, the classic defense of judicial power stems from the Founders' clear understanding that power, especially unchecked or unrestrained power, is inherently inimical to the principle of equal liberty. It is the "accumulation of all power into the same hands, whether of one, a few or many, and whether hereditary, self-appointed, or elective," that, Madison declared, could "justly be pronounced the very definition of tyranny."[2] If the Court could act as a check on the exercises of political power, as a "bulwark" and a "barrier" (in Hamilton's terms), it would serve well the Constitution's promise of a free democracy.[3]

The division of political power into separate departments, each with an interactive check on the other, was, first and foremost, a prophylactic device: hasty legislation, partial or unconstitutional legislation, illiberal, unjust, and tyrannical legislation would all be weeded out if the process of legislation involved the work of many agents, all of whom had a full or partial veto. "It will not be denied," Madison wrote in *The Federalist*, "that power is of an encroaching nature, and that it ought to be effectually restrained from passing the limits assigned to it."[4] Without the ability of each department to check the other, power would sooner or later accumulate in one place, threatening all freedom. In fact, it is the principle of separate, checking departments that Hamilton describes as one of the recent "improvements in the science of government" which made democracy finally supportable by the partisans of liberty.[5]

Thus the first argument not only for judicial review but for all checks and balances rests on this negative base: if power is dissipated and checked, liberty will flourish. Power checked meant liberty supported. Justice Louis D. Brandeis put this negative justification for checks forcefully and eloquently:

> The doctrine of the separation of powers was adopted by the Convention of 1787, not to promote efficiency but to preclude the exercise of arbitrary power. The purpose was not to avoid friction, but, by means of the inevitable friction incident to the distribution of governmental power among three departments, to save the people from autocracy.[6]

But this negative view of separation of powers is an insufficient view. The division of powers into distinct, interactive departments was meant to do more than merely protect the rights of the people from thoughtless or calculated abuse. There is a positive side to the principle of separation of powers which is all too often overlooked, especially in discussion of the role of the Court. "The importance of the Judiciary," General Charles C. Pinckney remarked at the Federal Convention, "will require men of the first talents...."[7] "First talents," to be sure, in order to help discern when the principles embodied in the Constitution were being violated; "first talents" to articulate the grounds on which the public or its representatives may have erred. But "first talents" also because those principles may well require more than defense. Principles—and the Constitution is replete with principles, ideas, theories—require learned application, understanding in changed circumstances, and serious thought as to their meaning, especially, as we shall see, to their meaning as they unfold themselves in time. "Judges," George Mason, Pinckney's colleague at the convention stated, "are in the habit and practice of considering laws in their true principles, and in all their consequences."[8] Here, at the level of consequence and true principle, on the level of contribution to political life rather than that of restrictions on political activity, is where the second, the more positive benefit of a separate judiciary emerges.

This position implies that the greatest role of the Court is not simply that it checks the unconstitutional transgressions of the legislative branch (as we noted earlier, the nation is so constructed as to mitigate that possibility as an ordinary occurrence, at least at the national level), but that it adds a dimension to public life that might otherwise be absent. The "chief worth" of the Court (as Cardozo said) is "in making vocal and audible the ideals that might otherwise be silenced, in giving them continuity of life and expression, in guiding and directing choice within the limits where choice ranges."[9] The primary defense, in other words, of the power of judicial review under the Constitution is the possibility of using that power as a guide to the democracy in its desire to live a principled life, a life in accord with certain formative national ideals. What is due process in today's situation? What does equal protection fully imply? To what new areas, now, do freedom of speech and freedom of the press extend? Without denying the necessity of oversight, without denying the appropriateness of negative checks on the Court as it pursues these ends in conjunction with democratic rule, we must recognize that is is here, in the sheltering and nourishing of ideals and principles and in the guidance of choice, that the supreme role of the Court is to be found.

The Supreme Court and the Development of American Principles

The Constitution is law. But it is also far more than law. The Constitution contains—one could almost say is—a theory of government, a formulation of principles, and an outline of procedures established to fulfill those principles. The questions that rightly come before the Court are questions more often of theory than of law narrowly conceived. They are questions of political and moral philosophy. And the branch to which we have, more than any other branch, entrusted the investigation of these questions must be, at its core, philosophic, devoted to reasoned inquiry and reasonable analysis. It is not simply a branch that checks for transgressions. This task of the Court—"to *evolve* and *apply*, although in a limited sphere, fundamental reasons of principle"—is the final, full defense of judicial review.[10]* This power is the positive good, rather than merely the negative check, that the idea of separation of powers, of separate qualities and capacities, has promised. It is this potential for the Court to be the institutionalized theoretician of the nation that gives meaning to the Madisonian dictum that, after separating the branches of power, we should then "collect the wisdom of its several parts."[11]

An oft-quoted remark by Henry M. Hart, Jr., captures clearly the essence of this judicial function: the Court is, he noted, "predestined in the long run not only by the thrilling tradition of Anglo-American law but also by the hard facts of its position in the structure of American institutions to be a voice of reason, charged with the creative function of discerning afresh and articulating and developing impersonal and durable principles."[12] More than a court of law, the Supreme Court needs to be a voice of reason, one that not only articulates and renews but also nourishes and develops our principles.

---

*In contrast to Ely (*Democracy and Distrust*), this chapter rests on two premises. First, that the Constitution is a preeminently principled document; it has in every part of its text a vision of ordered and equal liberty. To turn away from the principled nature of the Constitution and fit it instead into a procrustean bed of procedure alone is to mistake a part of the means for the end. Second, as a principled document it invites us to reason as to its application in every age: it encourages us to fashion arguments that persuade, based on the principles it espouses. To dismiss reasoning as the vehicle of understanding, as Ely does, is to leave us totally at sea (compare ibid., pp. 45–54, 56–60).

We must recognize that there is a strong sentiment, especially in those who share this book's concern regarding the limits as well as the scope of judicial power, to argue that all talk about a "living Constitution," growing and developing, is either faithlessness to the Constitution, pandering to the Court, or both. The Constitution (we are told) cannot change, except through amendments; and to argue that it can is simply a way of extending and illegitimately enhancing judicial power.

Yet, despite such objections, it is true, insofar as the Constitution embodies certain principles of justice and the just life, that the Constitution necessarily will develop. Such a position may or may not enhance judicial power.* But the way to limit the Court is not to limit the Constitution. To argue that ideas, including the ideas embedded in the text of our Constitution, necessarily grow and develop is not to deny the appropriateness or necessity, as we have seen them, of checks on the Court. But we must deny the value of attempting to limit the Court by limiting, by stunting, the development of the principles of equal liberty embodied in the Constitution. Fear of judicial supremacy should not lead us to deny to our national ideals of justice the right to fuller, newer, and deeper life. Despite our fears of judicial autocracy, we should not try to limit the Court by chaining the Constitution or by rejecting the Court's potentially most positive contribution: the ability to discern, articulate, and develop, with us, our still living fundamental constitutional principles.

The Growth of American Ideals

Principles are never static. They are born in time; they live, grow, and develop; and often they die. Like all living things,

---

*The most active Court in earlier American history, the anti–New Deal Court of the 1930s, proceeded on the assumption that the Constitution was essentially nondevelopmental. Contrary to some rather common opinion, we will not be able to restrict wide-ranging judicial activity merely by proclaiming the static nature of constitutional commands, remaining faithful to the historical meaning of the text, or demanding "strict construction."

they have the paradoxical capacity to grow and yet to remain the same simultaneously. One noted historian, reviewing the ideas the American colonists first enunciated, has remarked that our original colonial-revolutionary principles "turned in unfamiliar directions, towards conclusions [the colonists] could not themselves clearly perceive. They found a new world of political thought as they struggled to work out the implications of their beliefs."[13] As with all new and basic ideas, the same could be said of the growth and application of our founding constitutional principles—principles of freedom of speech and religion, of due process, of equal protection, of privacy, of, in brief, all the component parts of a life dedicated to the security and promotion of equal liberty. These ideas are among the most powerful of all our human forces. And it is part of the nature of the human species that we necessarily seek "to work out the implications" of our beliefs.

We should avoid here the danger of being too quick or too glib. To say, as legal scholars are often tempted to do, that the Constitution changes to meet our new and growing needs is to miss the point, and often to speak falsely. The point is not that our principles can change, under judicial guidance, in the sense that they then become wholly new. An overturning of principle is not what is contemplated here, and surely that type of change is not, under any circumstances, within the power of courts. Nor, on the other side, is it enough merely to say that our constitutional principles get new applications to new situations as they arise, that the Constitution can be stretched to cover new phenomena. Courts rightly do more than that. The greatest role of the Court is neither to revise our fundamental beliefs nor merely to apply those beliefs to new occurrences. At its peak the Court will be that part of American politics which more than any other struggles to work out the implications of our beliefs. More than any other branch the Court explains to us the living mute words of the Constitution as the Constitution's principles of equal liberty grow in self-understanding.

Perhaps it can be put this way: In the dialectic that ideas

have with life and experience, ideas themselves very often develop into fuller beings. Like children, ideas have a way of growing up, often growing in ways that their parents may not originally
have expected or foreseen. We now know, for example, perhaps
even better than Jefferson, the larger meaning of the notion
that all men are created equal. We have struggled with that idea
since its inception, watching it unfold to include blacks, women,
and others once only implicit in its meaning. We have seen, in
the great drama of American history, the idea of equal liberty
groping toward a wider understanding of itself, toward a life
without internal contradictions. Moreover, like Jefferson's ideal
of the equality of all men, such principles as freedom of speech
and of religion, equal protection, and due process have taken
deeper root and grown in new, unexpected, unforeseen directions. Here, in the reasoning out of our public philosophy, of
articulating the still shadowy images of our thoughts, is the final
justification for judicial review.

This position will immediately be opposed by those who demand that the Constitution be interpreted "historically," that it
be defined by reference to the "original intent" behind any particular phrase or part of the Constitution.* Although the intent
of the lawmaker is surely the law, a merely historical understanding of intent is incomplete. To define all principles only
by reference to the immediate concerns of their authors is to
hold that one knows a phenomenon sufficiently when one has
absorbed the genesis or the initial view of any particular idea.
But we can never fully grasp a living idea, never know it, by
ascribing its meaning, its full implication, its binding force to
the view of it held at its birth. Only after an idea is dead—no
longer believed in, no longer held—can it be known fully. The
meaning of "the rights of Englishmen," as the colonists soon
learned, could not be contained simply in the catalogue of rights

---

*The most forceful statement of this position in Raoul Berger's *Government
by Judiciary: The Transformation of the Fourteenth Amendment* (Cambridge: Harvard
University Press, 1977).

their British forebears recognized before the colonial crisis. The "rights of man" are not restricted to the rights enunciated in the climate of opinion of the eighteenth century. As John Adams said, "When a great question is first stated, there are very few, even of the greatest minds, which suddenly and intuitively comprehend it, in all its consequences."[14] Or, to return again to Lincoln, the idea enshrined in the Declaration of Independence, "that all men are created equal," was not meant to be a truth frozen within the boundaries of the history of its day but was intended as "a standard maxim for free society, which should be familiar to all, and revered by all, constantly looked to, constantly labored for, and even though never perfectly attained, constantly approximated, and thereby constantly spreading and deepening its influence."[15]*

It is in the very nature of ideas to grow in self-awareness, to work out all their implications over time. Merely to know the original content of an idea is partial and insufficient. As the ruling standard of American political development, the Constitution must be understood as including both permanence and change, but not understood as either static in its coverage or stunted in its meaning, bound by the history of its birth or fixed at the level of its original understanding.

This development of principles takes place in diverse ways. Often new circumstances, new events bring our constitutional principles to new levels of activity. The powers of Congress over

---

*In large measure the debate between Steven Douglas and Lincoln is a debate over the nature of interpretation, over the meaning of understanding. It was Douglas' view that one could find the correct interpretation of the principles of the Declaration of Independence by determining who was included within the scope of natural right at the time the document was written. To Douglas (and to Chief Justice Taney in Dred Scott) the true meaning of the principles of the Declaration was to be found in the "original understanding" of the document, by a process of freezing its meaning in time, by interpretation of the principles in terms of their original application to particulars. Lincoln understood, on the other hand, that principles can overcome their particular origins and their links to circumstance and can properly be seen as developmental, as never fully exhausted as long as people still subscribe to them and try to work out all their implications and applications.

commerce, for example, grew as commerce itself grew, reaching objects of commerce unknown to previous generations. The rights of speech and press have extended themselves to embrace new modes of communication. The idea expressed in the Constitution's prohibition against unreasonable searches could surely extend itself to cover the development of wiretapping.

On one level, then, the very content of the great clauses of the Constitution, their coverage, changes. And here the value, at least the potential value, of an institution that can judiciously consider the meaning, content, and coverage of our principles is evident. But the value—again the potential value—of a branch that has within its scope "capacities for dealing with matters of principle"[16] lies in its ability to aid us not only in the investigation of the coverage of our principles but especially in the understanding of their unfolding implications, their most profound meaning. The great phrases of the Constitution—due process, equal protection, even the guarantee of a republican form of government—are symbols of concepts that have, over time, consequences for political life beyond the most intelligent foresight of their framers.

Perhaps we can approach it in this manner: The Court in *Brown* v. *Board of Education* was wholly correct in seeing that the original understanding of the equal-protection clause as it might be elucidated by the history of the Fourteenth Amendment's ratification was not controlling.* Even if the formative under-

---

*The historical account, the Court decided, was not enough "to resolve the problem with which are faced." It was, at best, "inconclusive" (347 U.S. 483 [1954] 489). Consider in this regard James Madison's prescriptions regarding constitutional interpretation: Madison was against the publication of the debates that took place in the Federal Convention "till the Constitution should be well settled by practice. ... As a guide in expounding and applying the provisions of the Constitution, the debates and incidental decisions of the Convention can have no authoritative charter. ... [T]he legitimate meaning of the Instrument must be derived from the text itself" (Madison to Thomas Ritchie, September 15, 1821, in *Records of the Federal Convention*, ed. Farrand, 2:447; see also pp. 518, 521). It is the meaning of the ideas, not the particulars to which they were once attached, that we must first understand when we interpret the Constitution.

standing of that amendment was that segregated schools were indeed permissible, the truth is that, having worked out the inner logic of the meaning of "equal protection," we can rightly discover and proclaim that segregated schooling is *no longer* defensible. We can say that despite the "meaning" of the Fourteenth Amendment when it was written. To give another example, if the authors of our First Amendment did not presume that the principle of free speech implied the liberty of citizens to criticize their elected representatives, the reason can only be that the principle of free speech was still in its youth and needed time and thought to reach maturity. The inner logic of the Declaration's thesis that all men are created equal in rights necessarily means—once we begin to work it out—that black slavery is illegitimate, even if all the signers of that document were to have regarded their slaves as outside the principle.* The same is true, in our day, of the status of women under the equal protection clause: the principle of equality, in its drive to live

---

*I do not mean here to enter the dispute over whether Jefferson did or did not, by this phrase, have black slavery in mind or whether he was merely referring to Englishmen or to whites. Clearly, if my analysis is correct, the question loses much of its importance. For the record, however, I must say that I am persuaded that Jefferson could not have meant to exclude the black race from so sweeping a formulation. On this score, Lincoln's insights, partly quoted on p.148, seem convincing.

> This [the signers of the Declaration] said, and this they meant. They did not mean to assert the obvious untruth, that all were then actually enjoying that equality, nor yet, that they were about to confer it immediately upon them. In fact they had no power to confer such a boon. They meant simply to declare the *right*, so that the *enforcement* of it might follow as fast as circumstances should permit. They meant to set up a standard maxim for free society, which should be familiar to all, and revered by all; constantly looked to, constantly labored for, and even though never perfectly attained, constantly approximated, and thereby constantly spreading and deepening its influence, and augmenting the happiness and value of life to all people of all colors everywhere. [Lincoln, Speech at Springfield, June 26, 1857, in *Collected Works*, 2:405–6; emphasis, in original]

If this view is correct, the amazing thing is not that the signers of the Declaration had slaves but that they subscribed to a document that meant that they and their posterity were bound to free their slaves.

noncontradictorily, may lead us well beyond our original expectations.*

To summarize, the Constitution may properly develop in at least two ways. First, new items, new objects may come under the umbrella of old rules. Congress' power over commerce, for example, can grow to touch new objects, new commercial relations not in existence when the Constitution was written. Second, the ideas embodied in the constitutional text have, as do all ideas, the dynamic power of growth, the ability to work out all the implications of their own meaning.

We began this chapter with the negative conception of separation of powers as that division of political power necessary to prevent an illiberal concentration of power in any single institution. The right of judicial review and the appropriateness of checks on judicial review both have some sure basis in that fundamental political insight. But the power of judicial review—and, as we shall see, the necessity of its limitation—can also grow directly out of a more positive conception of separation of powers, one that sees the Court as particularly well suited to help us work out the meaning, the coverage, and the implications of our formative constitutional principles. If we begin with the separateness of the judiciary as an invitation for it contribute to the reasoned development of our ideals in an interactive manner with the other branches of democratic government, we can see an even grander purpose in the Founders' idea of separate powers, checked and balanced.

*Let me emphasize that we must exercise great care here. This defense of a developing Constitution does not mean to imply that the Constitution is "a living document," transforming its directives to meet our daily needs as a society, whatever those needs may be. The Constitution establishes certain principles, certain guides to action, political and personal. The argument here defended, that principles and ideas can develop, is not at all the same as pretending that the Constitution is a malleable document, shaping itself to fit the needs of contemporary society, as if the Constitution were mere flexibility itself, without principle, meaning, or solid purpose. More often than not—and with absolute propriety—society will be transformed as it follows the lead of its constitutional principles.

It bears repeating that this book's critique of judicial supremacy is not meant in derogation of judicial power or the function of judicial review. In fact, quite the opposite is intended: the more the Court can be treated as a partner in the politics of American life and not as a superior external agent, the fewer will be our doubts about its contributions and the greater should be our willingness to see it exercise its functions without misgivings. If the weakened principle of judicial self-restraint can be replaced by either formal or informal means of effective political partnership and interaction among the branches, that judicial activism which allows the Court openly to contribute its insights to the political process can grow and prosper. Adherence to the principle of external restraint would obviate much of the need for any reliance on the ineffective and sometimes inappropriate principles of self-restraint.[17]

Judicial Contributions to the Demands of a Free Society

Once we grasp the notion that ideas are necessarily developmental, and that their power over nations and people is strong and often unpredictable, we can affirm a greater but more problematic and difficult role for the Court in contemporary politics.

To the American Founders the preservation of liberty was intimately connected with the idea of restrictions on power, especially on political power. The more government was circumscribed, convoluted, and checked, the more might individual enterprise, private right, and personal liberty flourish. In the pursuit of this belief, as we have seen, the Founders set up a system of national democratic institutions that, in their intricacy and redundancy, could only rarely act in serious violation of the rights of individuals. Building on the Founders' desire to overcome the dangers of majoritarian despotism or legislative tyranny (yet retain "the spirit and form of popular government"), the American Constitution established an intricate, even baroque, system of self-government—staggered elections, bicameralism, separation of powers, checks and balances, federalism, written restrictions on political power.... All that human ingenuity could invent was fashioned by our forefathers in order to prevent hasty, ill-considered, or illiberal national legislation.

It was, of course, a system more prone to deadlock than to unseemly haste, more prone to compromise than to ideological purity. Since, in politics, some goods must often be sacrificed in order that others may be achieved, the goods of speed and righteous action were sacrificed in the name of pluralism, compromise, consensus, and political restraint. To repeat Madison's argument in *The Federalist*, "In the extended republic of the United States, and among the great variety of interests, parties and sects which it embraces, a coalition of a majority could seldom take place on any other principle than those of justice and the general good."[18]

The system was, on that level, nearly perfect. Madison was correct; the federal government that he and his colleagues bequeathed to us was only rarely, if ever, tyrannical. *It* did not enslave; *it* did not lower the wages of the laborer or extend the hours of the working poor. By comparison to the illiberal acts of individuals, corporations, and states, the national government was a paragon of liberal forbearance. The scheme of government devised by the Founders could indeed take the will of a democratic national majority and so refine it as to destroy any "common motive to invade the rights of other citizens."[19]

But ideas, as we have seen, are developmental. And the idea of liberty, as it grew, did not merely end with the demand for governmental restraint. As Americans soon came to see, liberty demanded not restraint but often a modicum of governmental activity; liberty needed to be not preserved and protected as much as it often needed to be promoted and expanded. Under the Founders' construct, the problem with American national government was not that it actively tyrannized but that, in the face of private oppressive acts, it often was ineffective or halting. Since it could rarely act except through consensus, the system had the potential to work as a shield for private, local varieties of exploitation.[20]

Yet, before we are tempted to turn to the courts to remedy the defects of congressional inaction, we must not falsify the historical record. In spite of the various brakes the Founders built into the legislative system, the litany of active, positive, and expansive congressional protection of the rights of all is a long one, beginning with all the great civil rights acts of Reconstruction and going through the Civil Rights Act of 1964, the Voting Rights Act of 1965, the Public Works Act of 1977, and scores of others. Nor should we forget that it was judges, not politicians, that after the Civil War most effectively destroyed Lincoln's legacy of human rights and equal liberty, that it was the courts that forced Congress to use the pretense of interstate commerce to protect the rights of blacks in this century because the courts had, on their own, effectively gutted the most expansive parts of the Fourteenth Amendment, and that, even as we praise *Brown* v. *Board*, we admit that what the Court overturned was not only restrictive state legislation but, more particularly, its own harsh formulation of the separate but equal doctrine in *Plessy*. The awful truth is that the political branches have too often been accused of the sins committed not by themselves but by our independently powerful judiciary. The current orthodoxy that sees congressional activity as little less than reactionary as it elevates the liberal character of judges and makes sacrosanct the decisions of the courts is both unfounded and misleading. The Court has often acted as a barrier not to national tyranny but rather to almost all national attempts to expand the meaning and scope of liberty in this country.[21]

Given this necessary reminder of the degree to which the Court has often retarded the expansion of civil liberties in this country, it remains true that the peculiar role the modern Court has taken on is less the rejection of national legislation in such areas as race relations or economics than the attempt to legislate for American society in new and affirmative ways.[22] The Court's particular task has been the wide and often highly problematic expansion of the meaning of equal liberty to new areas of race, alienage, gender, and status.[23] From an institution that once saw its overriding mission as restraining any legislative attempts to expand the meaning of the Constitution, today's Court fashions and refashions the meaning of our basic law seemingly at will.

In the course of this new activism the modern Court has blazed two separable yet equally important paths. The first and clearest path has been the vigorous extension of constitutional coverage to minor and disparate groups. The most obvious example remains the Warren Court's particular concern for the rights of the accused. But the most problematic endeavor of the modern Court has not really been its extensions of the Constitution to cover new groups but its expansion of the understanding, the meaning, of the various constitutional commands themselves.* As I argued earlier, ideas and principles have the capacity for self-reflection and, upon that reflection, the ability to grow. Under the aegis of the modern Court we have not only extended the applications but also grappled with the possible fuller meanings, the further implications, of a life dedicated to equality, to individual liberty, and to privacy. Does the equal protection clause, for example, forbid all types of racial discrimination? Does it forbid or does it sanction affirmative action policies based on color consciousness? To what degree does the same provision ban distinctions based on gender or age? Does the First Amendment's protection of freedom of speech reach certain varieties of nonverbal communication? Does it, in fact, reach particular types of actions and activities? Does the right to counsel include the right to supplied counsel? To what degree does the due process clause imply a "right" to certain social services and benefits? The catalogue of policy derivatives from general principles can be, has been, and will be expanded by the process of ongoing judicial deliberation.

---

*These activities are not mutually exclusive. The Burger Court's consistent expansion of the meaning of the equal protection clause to cover varieties of gender discrimination is a clear example of the extension of the coverage of old rules concomitant with an expansion of the meaning of those rules.

To say that ideas have consequences is true almost to the point of platitude. In the dialectic that ideas have with life and experience, both ideas and existence develop. To say that there is an institution that grapples with our deepest thoughts and explicates them is to say that that institution is the most politically important and pivotal institution in the land. To describe the Court as the "institutionalized theoretician" of the nation is not to insulate it in an ivory tower but to make it vastly strong. The principles of liberty and equality, the demands of community and privacy are central to our lives and indeed the lives of all nations, established or emergent. Any institution that has the power to elucidate and nourish these ideals is, by that very fact, uniquely powerful.

The Danger of Judicial Supremacy

Powerful, of course, for good or ill. These activities of the modern Court—the elucidation of our principles and the expansion of their coverage—comprise at once both the great promise and the great peril of judicial activism. The ability of the Court to reason through with us our principles is, potentially, the foremost contribution of judicial review. Without power we are diminished as a nation. But the power that comes from the authority to interpret for us our principles is also a power capable of doing serious and permanent harm. Because of this fact the reader will understand why this investigation has tried to elucidate the narrow line that separates judicial independence from judicial autocracy, why I have tried to place the Court within the necessary balance of separated and checked powers. That is, it is hardly seeking too much to ask that the power of judges be exercised under the partial oversight of the democracy they serve.

We have before us, then, the great paradox regarding judicial review: The Court's greatest promise is its potential to help us apply and develop our fundamental principles and constitutional commands, its ability, as we noted in Chapter 2, to help bring our philosophy to bear on our actions, to work out our present and our future in terms of our inheritance from the past. But that selfsame power contains within it the most serious of potential dangers, the possibility that the judiciary will substitute its principles for the Constitution's, and then actively enforce its visions autonomously and unchecked.

We know that the Court can make, and often has made, serious errors regarding the meaning and demands of the constitutional text. We know, that is, that the Court has stunted or tried to stifle the development of some of our living principles, that it has often retarded their growth, misconstrued their meaning, or denied their true implications. The racial cases of the 1880s, the economic decisions of the earlier part of this century, and the crisis of constitutional adjudication in the first years of the New Deal are obvious candidates for the title of serious constitutional mistakes, even if we look for our evidence only in the words and opinions of subsequent judicial decisions. More recently the Court's abortion decision in *Roe* v. *Wade* is a transparent attempt to impose a constitutionally unfounded policy preference on the unwilling words of the Constitution. And insofar as the Court's affirmative action decisions have reestablished race as a legitimate criterion for preference or reward, the Court has not expanded our highest constitutional principles but twisted them.

We cannot smugly attempt to sidestep the issue by denying that the Constitution can be erroneously interpreted, that interpretation is all a matter of opinion. Were that to be the case, we would pull the rug out from under the very rationale for judicial review. Because legislative mistakes and shortcomings are possible, judicial review has merit. Because *judicial* mistakes are possible, political interaction with the decisions of the Court is a necessity. Simple reverence for the Constitution (if not for the Court) requires that we not believe that the Constitution is all things the Supreme Court has sometimes claimed it is. By far the healthiest situation is that in which each of the three branches of American national politics can act both as a guide to and as a restraint on the others.*

As the powers of the judicial branch in the formation of public policy grow, the more clearly we should be aware at the outset of the various ways in which a fully independent and powerful judiciary can do both great good and real damage to the polity. It may, most obviously, crimp or stunt the ideals of American life. It may fully misinterpret the meaning of those principles. There is no reason why modern justices may not, as easily as did many of their predecessors, impose private views and personal ideologies regarding social or economic right on the constitutional text. It need not be Herbert Spencer's *Social Statics* that is read into constitutional law; it can just as easily be individual notions of abortion or of racial equity or of any particular vision of social justice. To cite Justice Frankfurter, "As history amply proves, the judiciary is prone to misconstrue the public good by confounding private notions with constitutional requirements."[24] Simple faith in the rightfulness of judicial rule may well give us not enduring principles but partisan ones.†

---

*Even as we recognize that the Court should be invited to contribute to the continual discussion of the meaning of our national principles, we must also understand that even that role will always be imperfect. Judges make no claims to be philosophers; they are (often at best) legal scholars. In other words, we should not forget Justice Robert Jackson's warning:

> Government by lawsuit leads to a final decision guided by the learning and limited by the understanding of a single profession—the law. ...[L]egal philosophy is but one branch of learning with peculiarities all its own and ... judicial review of the reasonableness of legislation means the testing of the whole social process by the single standard—of men of the Law [Robert Jackson, *The Struggle for Judicial Supremacy* (New York: Knopf, 1941), pp. 291–92]

Even Alexander Bickel was led, in his later work, to observe, "I have come to doubt in many instances the Court's capacity to develop 'durable principles' ... and to doubt, therefore, that judicial supremacy can work and is tolerable in broad areas of social policy" (*The Supreme Court and the Idea of Progress* [New York: Harper & Row, 1970], p. 99).

†Thinking low, one is tempted to repeat Jefferson's argument that both lawyers and judges have their own private interest in increasing the powers

Furthermore, the Court may go beyond mistaking the meaning of the Constitution: it may, almost as important, mistake the practical application of a principle. The principle of equal protection, to give one example, may well point to busing as a possible tool to be used in the destruction of the remnants of racial segregation. But if such a constitutional command results in "white flight" from urban areas and, in practice, debilitates the nation's cities or resegregates public schooling, then it is a prescription inexpediently proposed. These fears should not lead us to deny the potentially great contributions the Court can make within the tripartite system of power. The promise of the Court has always been its potential to be the voice of reason within a government almost wholly devoted to satisfying the demands of public constituencies. But this promise should not lead us to forget either the fallibility of judges as the reasoning element or the fact that principles are often necessarily incommensurate with developing circumstances and with the compromises demanded by political life in a pluralistic society.*

---

and prerogatives of the courts. In democratic elections each lawyer and each judge has one vote—a negligible impact on the direction of public policy. In a system of judicial governance active in the formation of public policy the power of individual judges and lawyers becomes immense. "One man, one vote" may be a good rule for the people; "one judge, ten million votes" is a rough approximation of the power of judges. But, as I said, only a person with the spirit of Jefferson would make so low an accusation.

*There is, of course, danger inherent in being *too* principled, failing to see that political life often demands hard compromises— if not compromises *of* principle, at least compromises *with* principle. Politics, at least democratic politics, often requires the use of principles as goals and not always as rules of immediate action (see Horowitz, *Courts and Social Policy*, chap. 2, especially pp. 51–56, and Cox, *Role of the Supreme Court*, pp. 93–96). Bickel sought to have the Court sidestep the problem of overprincipledness by reference to techniques that allowed the Court to avoid making principled constitutional decisions (*Least Dangerous Branch*, pp. 111–98; but see Gerald Gunther, "The Subtle Vices of the Passive Virtues: A Comment on Principle and Expediency in Judicial Review," *Columbia Law Review* 64 [January 1964]:25). The essence of statemanship is the old virtue of prudence, the ability to combine the rule of just principles with due regard for the demand of circumstance. The greatest courts are those that act statesmanly as well as judicially, developing with us

The demands of the present and the desires of each age deserve to be guided by principle. Partly for that reason the Court was separated from the other branches of power and given secure status. But the necessities of the present are generally known best to the more political branches, and therein lies a central reason not for the rigid separation of powers but for their ultimate interaction. The American polity is, at its peak, a mixture of both wisdom, or true principles, and consent, or the democratic will. It takes no great insight to see that these objectives coexist in some tension. But it still remains true that the mixture of both, not the supremacy of either alone, was the goal of the Founders of our mixed and balanced government. How do we, as a nation, give the Court the power and opportunity to guide us through our living and developing Constitution and still prevent the Court from substituting its principles of the Constitution, and elevating its rule over ours? In that question is the whole tangled problem this book has sought to unroll.

The attempt made in this book to help us view the Court again as a partner in constitutional interpretation and not as its final arbiter takes on additional importance in the particular context of the judicial activism of today. As I argued from the start of this book, it can no longer be said that judicial review is a negative power only, that "the Court can forbid someone else to act but cannot, usually, act itself."[25] In former times, when judicial activism meant the overturning of the democratic wish expressed in terms of general public policy, everyone knew, unless the democracy was persuaded by the Court, that in time the Court would lose. Time and death, in league with presidential selection, would usually suffice. An active Court that crossed vital national interests was a difficulty, a stumbling block, but not an insurmountable obstacle. The Court could be waited

---

our principles, working out the implications of our ideas, and finding appropriate ways to invite us to live in the fullness of equal liberty.

out. Its finality, in other words, was, in years past, not so final. But judicial finality has a harder punch today. Again, the hallmark of modern activism is less the denial of right or power, the brake on acts and actions, than the general judicial conferral of powers and rights. It is hardly uncommon for judicial decisions in these areas to involve the establishment of new public programs, the initiation of new privileges and procedures, and the expenditure of large sums of money.[26] As we noted in the first chapter, a "checking" Court might well always lose to the forces of democracy in time; but a Court that takes upon itself the power of advancing new vistas of right is not fighting those rear-guard losing battles of years past. Or, as one judicial scholar recently wrote: "It is no longer even approximately accurate to say that courts exercise only a veto. What is asked and what is awarded is often the doing of something, not just the stopping of something."[27] And it is clearly more difficult to restrict a body that, under the guise of finality, is making policy, legislating in a direct way, rather than a body that merely checks the legislation of others.

To the degree that we have reached the point where judges truly can legislate, judge, and execute their opinions autonomously, unchecked, the situation is manifestly no longer tolerable. Insofar as the contemporary view of the judiciary as irresponsible—possessing policy-making independence coupled with finality regarding its own decisions—is even close to the truth, we have undermined both the spirit of republican government and the idea of constitutionalism itself—the very idea that gave judicial review its birth.

Conclusion

We have reached the crossroads in the history of judicial power. We now know, better than our forefathers, that the great principle of American liberty often requires not merely political abstention from the cares and tribulations of life, a laissez-faire attitude toward social and economic difficulties, but the positive, active involvement of the force of government in various areas of human endeavor. We know that the deliberate and often cumbersome arrangements of legislative institutions in America, designed to prevent hasty, ill-considered, or illiberal acts, are sometimes too slow and often unable to remedy the denial of rights and privileges to certain individuals, groups, and classes.* We also know that part of the importance of the modern Court has been its ability to extend the idea of liberty into areas previously untouched by the process of ordinary legislative politics. In a number of areas, the modern Court has legislated liberty for us.

Yet the selfsame power of the courts to remedy for us a wide variety of errors and shortcomings is hardly an unambiguous good. We must, of course, go further than to signal our concern over particular acts of modern judicial policy. To write a detailed critique of the manifest errors of judicial legislation in the field of abortion or criminal rights or racial policy would be as easy as it would be tedious. It is the very power and scope of modern judicial review that is both its greatness and its main danger to American life, not any single decision or particular line of cases.

---

*Insofar as liberty means being left alone, unhampered by governmental interference in the millions of life's choices and mistakes, fewer nations have ever been freer than America. But insofar as liberty is held to include freedom from the domination and direction of nongovernmental forces—economic powers, "superior" racial or religious groups, and so on—a different historical tally is possible. Liberty truly may also include freedom from the forces of circumstance, accident, and nature—ill health, disease, poverty, old age. Americans have always clearly understood that power is the perennial antagonist of liberty. But our general tendency has been to see power primarily as governmental power rather than as private or natural power. Thus, especially before the rise of New Deal liberalism, we have hesitated to use governmental power to free individuals from the power of nonpolitical forces. That we were, indeed, the last of the great nations to eliminate the private selling of human beings (and there extraconstitutionally) and among the last to institute social policies in such areas as education, industry, agriculture, and health bespeaks the difficulty we have in seeing liberty, first, as a growing concept, and second, as more than merely restrictions on political power. Needless to say, this footnote could well be a volume in itself.

We must ask ourselves, if judicial review is a means to check legislative encroachments, what means exist to check the encroachments of the judiciary, a judiciary that has increasingly taken on itself the attributes and powers of legislation? What checks can we devise in order to superintend a judiciary with (it is claimed) final power over policies involving abortion, welfare, schools, police, racial balance, busing, employment? The proclamation of judicial review as the nation's security against anticonstitutional abuses rings hollow unless we give some thought to the problem of unreviewed judicial legislation as well. The same arguments that have led us to support judicial review—its defense of constitutional government and its ability to block the unwarranted exercise of independent power—should lead us to worry about the ever-growing power of judges to shape public policy on their own authority, unchecked. In other words, it is the wide-ranging ability of the Court to extend the coverage and latent meaning of our principles that is both the clear promise and the great peril of modern judicial activism.

The liberties of subjects, it used to be said, were endangered more by good kings than by bad. Good kings tended to accumulate powers without objection; bad kings inherited those powers to use any way they chose. On one side, American liberal opinion has been agreeable to the expansion of judicial activity, despite its undemocratic nature, because the modern judiciary has tended, in some areas, toward the expansion of liberty and equality as it increased its own authority. But insofar as the Court has taken upon itself, unchecked, legislative and executive attributes in the positive formation of public policy, insofar as the Court has been a leader in the making and enforcement of societal rules, the concerns of those who decry the dangers of judicial imperialism can no longer be lightly dismissed.

Perhaps we should give the last few words to the Founders. Although they may not have foreseen the full flowering of the principles and institutions they set in motion, the Founders wisely knew the precondition necessary for the ultimate preservation of our liberal institutions. They knew, that is to say, "that whatever power in any government is independent, [such a power] is absolute also."[28] They knew the dangers of coalescing political power in the same hands.[29] Though Hamilton may have predicted that the courts would be "the weakest of the three departments of power," the branch "least dangerous to the political rights of the Constitution" and least dangerous to "the general liberty of the people," that prediction was offered only insofar as the courts remained substantially removed from the general process of policy formation. "Though individual oppressions may now and then proceed from the courts of justice, the general liberty of the people can never be endangered from that quarter: I mean so long as the judiciary remains truly distinct from both the legislative and the executive."[30] Or, to rephrase these remarks yet keep their sense, liberty will be secure so long as the judiciary, no matter how fair it may seem to be, does not subsume legislative and executive powers under its own jurisdiction, exercising those powers without effective external check.

In his comments Hamilton obviously had in mind the fear that the representative branches would subvert the independence of the courts. But the same principle is at work if the courts absorb and wield the functions of the other branches.* To refer to the argument made in Chapter 2 of this book, judicial supremacy no less than legislative omnipotence is an attack on the very idea of constitutional government. In truth, the perils of judicial supremacy are actually much worse than

---

*"Were the power of judging joined with the legislative, the life and liberty of the subject would be exposed to arbitrary control, for *the judge* would then be *the legislator*. Were it joined to the executive power, *the judge* might behave with all the violence of *an oppressor*" (*Federalist*, no. 47, p. 326; quoting Montesquieu). Students of contemporary America can perhaps sharpen their feeling for the Founders' concern over checks and balances by considering that the fundamental constitutional defect of the Nixon administration was that it was becoming substantially unchecked—it was waging war, impounding funds, and conducting surveillances on the basis of its own will (i.e., the legislative power) and executing that will autonomously. It was only the oversight, the check, of the other two branches working in concert that undermined this type of illicit independence.

those of unchecked legislative omnipotence. The fact is that Congress can work only through compromise and under the elective oversight of the voting public. Though neither of those checks is sufficient for good government, they are more than we generally have over judicial decisions.

It therefore bears repeating that the Court's new activist role points us more urgently than ever not to the denial of judicial power but toward the discovery of ways again to mesh the idea of judicial power with some effective process of mutual oversight and review. The function of the Court is to nurture our fundamental principles and reform democratic opinion. But it may not, in the end, either consider those principles a property wholly its own or supplant the opinion of the public as the ruling element in the nation.

Throughout this book, the question has never been "Within government where should constitutional supremacy be?" Our government was to be a government of *shared* powers—shared in the process of legislation and shared in the shaping of the Constitution into particular formulations. This argument has been designed not to reduce the Court but to raise it up to the level of partnership in a government whose parts are both separated and overlapping. When we look at the various branches of national power we should see that the answer to the question "Who governs?" must remain "*They* govern. All of them."

We have entered a new age with the modern Court. Unlike its older activist predecessors, the Court is not antilegislative but itself legislative. No number of scholarly tracts describing the virtues of judicial self-restraint will stay the Court from increasing its work in those areas where it decides work is to be done. In fact, the old doctrine of judicial restraint seems clearly to have fallen on hard times. As an attempt to minimize the chilling effect of final judicial decisions on democratic life, the principle of judicial restraint was an effort well directed but futile. The limitations of the doctrine lay not with its perception of the problem—the problem of a final court in the midst of a democratic society—but in its solution, the belief that people will

restrain themselves. Moreover, insofar as the doctrine of restraint tended to restrict the Court from entering those areas
of civil and political injustice in which the judiciary was able to
frame reasonable remedies where no one else would act, self-
restraint deprived the whole nation of potentially valuable judicial contributions. But if fear of mistake—fear of finality—
induces a desire for restraint, then the answer is to elucidate
ways to restore the Court to the active partnership of checks
and balances, and not to ask it to be passive.

Such restoration in practice might allow us to put aside our
hesitancy about the active exercise of judicial review and to see
judicial review not primarily as a restriction on democratic life[31]
but as a positive invitation to a democratic response. Clearly,
judicial activism, understood as the liberty of judges to act on
their own desires and personal views, is unquestionably indefensible. And that restraint which is "rooted in a respect for the
dignity and high purposes of the other branches of government
and a sympathetic understanding of the problems they must try
to resolve" is an absolute prerequisite for any intelligent constitutional interpretation.[32] But that activism which allows the
Court to propound its constitutional and legal conviction
openly—that activism which does not fear to make "vocal and
audible the ideals that might otherwise be silenced"—is the very
contribution promised us by the power of judicial review.[33] That
promise—that chance always to speak, as Lincoln once said, to
"the better angels of our nature"—is a promise that should not
be abandoned.[34]

Yet only through a solid understanding that the principle
of checks and balances is a partnership and not simply a donation of power to the Court can we actively defend ourselves
against the potential dangers of an active Court. Only through
a reinvigoration of the political interaction of all branches of
power can the vision of a Court engaged in a "continuing col-
loquy with the political institutions and with society at large" be
fully realized. And only in this way will there then exist "principle evolved conversationally, not perfected unilaterally."[35]

We end on much the same note with which we began: There is an inherent tension in any society that seeks to combine democracy, constitutionalism, and judicial review. The normal instinct to resolve the tension, to make either the immediate desires of the democracy or the will of a select and permanent judiciary the paramount governing force, should be resisted. The genius of the system lies in the very tension itself, and in our ability to combine an active democracy, constitutional principles, and judicial judgment. If this book can serve as a guide to the complexity of the problem and as a preface to further practical suggestions, it will have fulfilled its mission.

Notes

Epigraphs: Brewer quoted in Edward S. Corwin, *Twilight of the Supreme Court* (New Haven: Yale University Press, 1934), p. xxv; "Constitutional Interpretation: An Interview with Justice Lewis Powell," *Kenyon Alumni Bulletin* 3, no. 3 (Summer 1979):15.

Preface

1. C. Herman Pritchett, "Judicial Supremacy from Marshall to Burger," in *Essays on the Constitution of the United States*, ed. M. Judd Harmon (Port Washington, N.Y.: Kennikat Press, 1978), p. 111.

2. Nathan Glazer, "Towards an Imperial Judiciary?" *Public Interest*, Fall 1975, pp. 104–23.

3. J. Skelly Wright, "The Role of the Supreme Court in a Democratic Society," *Cornell Law Review* 54 (1968):3.

4. The literature describing the new imperial judiciary is large. Archibald Cox, "The New Dimensions of Constitutional Adjudication," *Washington Law Review* 51 (1976):791–829, is an early comprehensive and critical piece. See also Donald L. Horowitz, *The Courts and Social Policy* (Washington, D.C.: Brookings Institution, 1977), and Glazer, "Towards an Imperial Judiciary?"

5. Chief Justice Harlan Stone refers to the use of judicial power as a "sober second thought" in "The Common Law in the United States," *Harvard Law Review* 50 (1936):25.

6. John Hart Ely, *Democracy and Distrust* (Cambridge: Harvard University Press, 1980), pp. 87, 74.

7. Ibid., p. 102.

8. Jesse H. Choper, *Judicial Review and the National Political Process* (Chicago: University of Chicago Press, 1980), pp. 2, 68, 69.

1   The Limits of Judicial Power

Epigraphs: Jefferson to Madison, March 15, 1789, in *The Papers of Thomas Jefferson*, ed. Julian Boyd et al., 20 vols. to date (Princeton: Princeton University Press, 1950–), 14:659; Jefferson, "Autobiography," in *The Writings of Thomas Jefferson*, ed. Andrew A. Lipscomb, 20 vols. (Washington, D.C.: Thomas Jefferson Memorial Association, 1904–5), 1:121.

1. *The Federalist*, ed. Jacob E. Cooke (Middletown, Conn.: Wesleyan University Press, 1961), no. 78, pp. 526, 522. A contemporary restatement of this general position may be found in Raoul Berger, *Congress v. the Supreme Court* (Cambridge: Harvard University Press, 1969), chap. 6, especially pp. 193–99.

2. United States v. Butler, 297 U.S. 1, 62 (1936).

3. Marbury v. Madison, 1 Cranch 137 (1803), 177, 180.

4. *Federalist*, no. 81, p. 544.

5. Ibid., no. 78, p. 528.

6. *Federalist*, no. 78, pp. 529, 523.

7. The seminal and still paramount article in this area is Eugene V. Rostow, "The Democratic Character of Judicial Review," *Harvard Law Review* 66 (December 1952):193–224; see especially sec. III, pp. 203–10, 215. See also Charles L. Black, *The People and the Court* (Englewood Cliffs, N.J.: Prentice-Hall, 1960), pp. 87–119, and J. Skelly Wright, "The Role of the Supreme Court in a Democratic Society," *Cornell Law Review* 54 (November 1968):1–28.

8. Jefferson to Madison, March 15, 1789, in *Papers of Thomas Jefferson*, 14:659.

9. *Annals of Congress* (1st Cong., 1st sess.), 1:439.

10. 1 Cranch 137 (1803), 179.

11. Rostow, "Democratic Character," p. 215.

12. The phrase is Hamilton's, in *Federalist*, no. 78, p. 523.

13. Ibid., no. 51, pp. 352–53.

14. The phrase "auxiliary precautions" is also in *Federalist*, no. 51, p. 349. That paper contains the best summary of these precautions, the principles animating them, and the goals that inspired their invention.

15. James B. Thayer, "The Origin and Scope of the American Doctrine of Constitutional Law," *Harvard Law Review* 7 (October 1893):137. This observation did not, of course, originate with Thayer. See, for one example, the speech of Congressman Israel Smith (Vermont) in *Annals of Congress* (7th Cong., 1st sess.), 11:698–99.

16. Dred Scott v. Sandford, 19 Howard 393 (1857); United States v. Reese, 92 U.S. 214 (1876); United States v. Cruikshank, 92 U.S. 542 (1876); United States v. Harris, 106 U.S. 629 (1883); The Civil Rights Cases, 109 U.S. 3 (1883); Adair v. United States, 208 U.S. 161 (1908); Hammer v. Dagenhart, 247 U.S. 251 (1918); Bailey v. Drexel Furniture Co., 259 U.S. 20 (1922); Adkins v. Children's Hospital, 261 U.S. 525 (1923). For sober reviews of many of these cases, see Edward S. Corwin, *Court over Constitution* (Princeton: Princeton Uni-

versity Press, 1938), pp. 85–128, and Henry Steele Commager, "Judicial Review and Democracy," *Virginia Quarterly Review* 10 (1938):417–28.

17. Hammer v. Dagenhart, 247 U.S. 251 (1918).

18. Bailey v. Drexel Furniture Co., 259 U.S. 20 (1922).

19. United States v. Darby, 312 U.S. 100 (1941).

20. Leonard W. Levy, "Judicial Review, History, and Democracy," in *Judicial Review and the Supreme Court*, ed. Levy (New York: Harper & Row, 1967), pp. 33–34. The pages that follow this statement contain the most powerful nonpolemical indictment of the Court's activities in the realm of personal rights and civil liberties to be found anywhere in modern judicial literature.

21. John G. Frank, "Review and Basic Liberties," in *Supreme Court and Supreme Law*, ed. Edmond Cahn (Bloomington: Indiana University Press, 1954), p. 112.

22. Levy, "Judicial Review," p. 36.

23. *Federalist*, no. 10, p. 64; no. 51, p. 353.

24. Abraham Lincoln, "First Inaugural Address," in *The Collected Works of Abraham Lincoln*, ed. Roy P. Basler, 9 vols. (New Brunswick, N.J.: Rutgers University Press, 1953), 4:268.

25. Jefferson, "First Inaugural Address," in *The Writings of Thomas Jefferson*, ed. Andrew A. Lipscomb, 20 vols. (Washington, D.C.: Thomas Jefferson Memorial Association, 1905), 3:318.

26. Rostow, "Democratic Character," p. 199.

27. Benjamin N. Cardozo, *The Nature of the Judicial Process* (New Haven: Yale University Press, 1921), p. 93.

28. Robert Dahl, "Decision Making in a Democracy: The Supreme Court as National Policy Maker," *Journal of Public Law* 6 (1958):285. See also pp. 288 and 291.

29. Jack W. Peltason, *Federal Courts in the Political Process* (New York: Random House, 1955), p. 63.

30. Dahl, "Decision Making," p. 293.

31. Glazer, "Towards an Imperial Judiciary?" p. 106.

32. Max Farrand, ed., *The Records of the Federal Convention of 1787*, 4 vols. (New Haven: Yale University Press, 1966), 2:299.

33. *Federalist*, no. 78, p. 523.

34. Black, *People and the Court*, pp. 115, 117. See also pp. 178–82 and 209–11.

35. The best statement of this position still remains Alexander Bickel, *The Least Dangerous Branch: The Supreme Court at the Bar of Politics* (Indianapolis: Bobbs-Merrill, 1962).

36. A. F. of L. v. American Sash Door Co., 335 U.S. 538 (1949), 555; Minersville v. Gobitis, 310 U.S. 586 (1940), 600; West Virginia Board of Education v. Barnette, 319 U.S. 624 (1943), 650. Justice Powell warned of "the countermajoritarian implications of judicial review" (United States v. Richardson, 418 U.S. 166 [1974], 192). See also Bickel, *Least Dangerous Branch*, pp. 16–23.

37. Tom Paine, "Common Sense," in *The Complete Writings of Thomas Paine*, ed. Philip S. Foner, 2 vols. (New York: Citadel Press, 1945), 1:6.

38. Baron de Montesquieu, *Considerations on the Causes of the Greatness of the*

Romans and Their Decline, trans. David Lowenthal (Ithaca: Cornell University Press, 1965), pp. 93–94.

2 *Judicial Review and the Rise of Constitutional Government*

Epigraph: Sam Adams, *The Writings of Sam Adams*, ed. H. A. Cushing, 4 vols. (New York: Putnam, 1903–8), 3:262.

1. James Otis, "Speech on the Writs of Assistance," February 24, 1761, in *The Works of John Adams*, ed. Charles F. Adams, 10 vols. (Boston: Little, Brown, 1850–56), 2:522.

2. John Adams to William Tudor, March 29, 1817, in ibid., 10:248. See also 10:183–84 and 232–34.

3. Adams to William Wirt, January 2, 1818, in ibid., 10:272.

4. Dr. Bonham's Case, 8 Rep. 118a (C.P. 1610).

5. For a discussion of Holt and Hobart, see Berger, *Congress v. the Supreme Court*, pp. 24–26.

6. William Blackstone, *Commentaries on the Laws of England*, ed. Edward Christian, 4 vols. (Boston: T. B. Wart, 1818), 1:90.

7. "The Rights of the British Colonies Asserted and Proved," *Boston Gazette*, July 23, 1764, reprinted in *Tracts of the American Revolution, 1763–1776*, ed. Merrill Jensen (Indianapolis: Bobbs-Merrill, 1967), pp. 19–40.

8. Bernard Bailyn, ed., *Pamphlets of the American Revolution, 1750–1776* (Cambridge: Belknap Press of Harvard University Press, 1965), p. 414.

9. Thomas Hutchinson to Richard Jackson, September 12, 1765, in ibid., p. 413.

10. Edward S. Corwin, *The "Higher Law" Background of American Constitutional Law* (Ithaca: Cornell University Press, 1928, 1955), pp. 77–78.

11. Berger, *Congress v. the Supreme Court*, p. 27n.

12. See Bernard Bailyn, *The Ideological Origins of the American Revolution* (Cambridge: Harvard University Press, 1967), pp. 67–68, 175–98; Gordon Wood, *The Creation of the American Republic* (Chapel Hill: University of North Carolina Press, 1969), pp. 259–68.

13. John Joachim Zubly, "Humble Enquiry" (1769), quoted in Bailyn, *Ideological Origins*, pp. 181-82.

14. Thomas Jefferson, "Notes on the State of Virginia," in *Writings of Thomas Jefferson*, 2:160.

15. Demophilus [pseud.], "The Genuine Principles of the Anglo-Saxon or English Constitution" (1776), quoted in Bailyn, *Ideological Origins*, pp. 183–84.

16. *Writings of Thomas Jefferson*, 2:165.

17. *Writings of Sam Adams*, 3:262.

18. "Return of the Town of Concord," October 22, 1776, in *The Popular Source of Political Authority: Documents on the Massachusetts Constitution of 1780*, ed. Oscar Handlin and Mary Handlin (Cambridge: Belknap Press of Harvard University Press, 1966), pp. 152–53.

19. The history of these bodies and of the acts found to be unconstitutional by them is discussed in Charles Grove Haines, *The American Doctrine of Judicial Supremacy*, rev. and enl. ed. (New York: Russel & Russel, 1959), pp. 82–85.

20. Carl J. Friedrich, *Constitutional Government and Democracy* (Boston: Ginn, 1950), p. 26. For a full exposition of this aspect of constitutionalism, see all of chap. 1, pp. 5–36.

3   The Growth of Judicial Power

1. For a good summary of this case, Trevett v. Weeden, see Haines, *American Doctrine*, pp. 109–12, and William W. Crosskey, *Politics and the Constitution*, 2 vols., (Chicago: University of Chicago Press, 1953), 2:965–68.

2. Haines, *American Doctrine*, p. 109.

3. Crosskey, *Politics and the Constitution*, 2:968.

4. For a full discussion of this case, Rutgers v. Waddington (New York, 1784), see Haines, *American Doctrine*, pp. 98–104, and Crosskey, *Politics and the Constitution*, 2:968–70.

5. Haines, *American Doctrine*, pp. 92–95; Crosskey, *Politics and the Constitution*, 2:948–52.

6. Farrand, ed., *Records of the Federal Convention*, 1:97.

7. Ibid., 1:109 (King); 2:73 (Wilson); 2:78 (Mason); 2:440 (Madison); 2:299 (Morris); 2:376 (Williamson); 2:76 (Martin).

8. Ibid., 2:93.

9. Ibid., 2:298 (Mercer) and 299 (Dickinson).

10. The original plan for the council of revision is in ibid., 1:21.

11. *Federalist*, no. 78, p. 523.

12. Ibid., pp. 523–24.

13. Ibid., p. 525.

14. Ibid., no. 81, pp. 545–46.

15. Hylton v. United States, 3 Dallas 171 (1796). This case predates Marbury by seven years.

16. See Jonathan Elliot, *Debates in the Several State Conventions on the Adoption of the Federal Constitution*, 5 vols. (Philadelphia: Lippincott, 1861), 4:532–39.

17. 5 U.S. (1 Cranch) 137 (1803), 176–80.

18. Ibid., p. 177.

19. See Bickel, *Least Dangerous Branch*, pp. 1–14, and Archibald Cox, *The Role of the Supreme Court in American Government* (New York: Oxford University Press, 1976), pp. 12–14.

20. 1 Cranch 137 (1803), 177, 180, 176.

21. 1 Cranch 137 (1803), 180.

22. *Federalist*, no. 78, p. 526.

23. 1 Cranch 137 (1803), 180.

24. Variants of this argument may be found in Cox, *Role of the Supreme Court*, pp. 14–15, and in Herbert Wechsler, "Toward Neutral Principles of Constitutional Law," in *Principles, Politics, and Fundamental Law* (Cambridge: Harvard University Press, 1961), pp. 7–9. Cf. Louis H. Pollak, "Racial Discrimination and Judicial Integrity: A Reply to Professor Wechsler," *University of Pennsylvania Law Review* 108 (1959):2–3, and Bickel, *Least Dangerous Branch*, pp. 8, 11–12.

25. Art. III, sec. 2.

26. 1 Stat. 73, 85–86.

27. *Federalist*, no. 51, p. 349.

28. Ibid., no. 48, p. 332. See also no. 73, p. 495.

29. Jefferson to George Wythe, July 1776, in *Writings of Thomas Jefferson*, 4:258–59. See also Farrand, *Records of the Federal Convention*, 2:73–80, especially Madison's speech, p. 77, and Wilson's and Morris's comments, p. 78.

4   From Judicial Review to Judicial Supremacy

Epigraph: James Madison, "Observations on Jefferson's Draft of a Constitution for Virginia" (1788), in *The Writings of James Madison*, ed. Gaillard Hunt, 9 vols. (New York: Putnam, 1900–1910), 5:294.

1. 4 Wheat. 316 (1819); 9 Wheat. 1 (1824).

2. Jefferson to Madison, March 15, 1789, in *Papers of Thomas Jefferson*, 14:659.

3. Elliot, *Debates*, 4:528, 529, 532. The texts of both resolutions are given in ibid., 4:528–32 and 540–45.

4. *Federalist*, no. 15, p. 93.

5. Farrand, ed., *Records of the Federal Convention*, 3:537.

6. *Federalist*, no. 78, p. 523. Hamilton is here quoting Montesquieu, as he notes.

7. Jefferson to Abigail Adams, July 22, 1804, in *Writings of Thomas Jefferson*, 11:43–44

8. *Writings of Thomas Jefferson*, 5:213, 220, 298, 276. These statements are from letters written by Jefferson in 1819 and 1820.

9. Jefferson to Adamantios Coray, October 31, 1823, in ibid., 15:487.

10. Jefferson to W. H. Torrance, June 11, 1815, in ibid., 14:303, 305.

11. See Elliot, *Debates*, 4:532–39.

12. Daniel Webster, "Speech on the Presidential Veto" (July 11, 1832) in *The Great Speeches and Orations of Daniel Webster*, ed. Edwin P. Whipple (Boston: Little, Brown, 1889), p. 330. See also "Reply to Hayne" (January 26 and 27, 1830), p. 265, and "Reply to Calhoun" (February 16, 1833), p. 282.

13. Dred Scott v. Sandford, 19 Howard 393 (1857), 451.

14. Lincoln, Sixth Debate at Quincy, October 13, 1858, in *Collected Works*, 3:267. The complete debates are in ibid., 3:1–325.

15. Douglas' reply to Lincoln, Third Debate, at Jonesboro, September 15, 1858, in Lincoln, *Collected Works*, 3:142–43.

16. Douglas' reply to Lincoln, Fifth Debate, at Galesburg, October 7, 1858, in ibid., p. 243. See also pp. 112 and 267–68.

17. Quoted by Lincoln in his speech at Springfield, June 26, 1857, in ibid., 2:401.

18. Lincoln, speech at Springfield, July 17, 1858, in ibid., p. 516.

19. Lincoln, First Inaugural Address, March 4, 1861, in ibid., 4:268.

20. James D. Richardson, ed., *Messages and Papers of the Presidents* (Washington, D.C.: Government Printing Office, 1896), 2:581–82. See Lincoln, *Collected Works*, 2:402–3, 496.

21. Lincoln, speech at Springfield, July 17, 1858, in *Collected Works*, 2:516,

and Douglas' speech, Third Debate, at Jonesboro, September 15, 1858, in ibid., 3:112. See also ibid., 3:267–68.

22. Lincoln, First Inaugural Address, March 4, 1861, in ibid., 4:268.

23. Bickel, *Least Dangerous Branch*, pp. 24–25.

24. Lincoln, speech at Springfield, July 17, 1858, in *Collected Works*, 2:516.

25. Marbury v. Madison, 1 Cranch 137 (1803), 179–80; emphasis in original.

26. Bickel, *Least Dangerous Branch*, pp. 3–4.

27. Jefferson to William Charles Jarvis, September 28, 1820, in *Writings of Thomas Jefferson*, 15:276.

5 *"From This Court There Is No Appeal"*

Epigraph: Robert Yates, "Letters of Brutus," no. 11, in *The Antifederalists*, ed. Cecelia M. Kenyon (Indianapolis: Bobbs-Merrill, 1966), p. 338. See also pp. lxxxvii–lxxxviii, 25, 323. Yates went to Philadelphia as a member of the New York delegation to the Constitutional Convention in 1787, but returned to New York in July. He refused to sign the completed Constitution and strenuously opposed its adoption. His "Letters of Brutus" may well be the most perceptive of all the antifederalist tracts.

1. *Federalist*, no. 78, p. 523.

2. Ibid., no. 81, p. 542.

3. Ibid., no. 47, p. 324.

4. Ibid., no. 48, p. 332. The whole of this paper and the one that precedes it are vital for any understanding of checks and balances.

5. Ibid., p. 332.

6. *Writings of Thomas Jefferson*, 4:258–59.

7. *Federalist*, no. 47, p. 325; emphasis in original.

8. Ex parte Grossman, 267 U.S. 87 (1925), 119–20 (Taft, C. J.).

9. 1 Cranch 137 (1803), 176.

10. Cooper v. Aaron, 358 U.S. 1 (1958), 17.

11. Brown v. Allen, 344 U.S. 450 (1953).

12. United States v. Butler, 297 U.S. 1 (1936), 78–79.

13. 358 U.S. 1 (1958), 17.

14. 1 Cranch 137 (1803), 178. See the analysis of constitutionalism in chap. 2 above.

15. Robert Scigliano, *The Supreme Court and the Presidency* (New York: Free Press, 1971), p. 55.

16. Marbury v. Madison, 1 Cranch 137 (1803), 177.

17. *Federalist*, no. 58, p. 397.

18. The seminal article regarding modern concepts of judicial restraint is Thayer, "Origin and Scope." Bickel's *Least Dangerous Branch* is the major contemporary restatement of this position.

19. *Federalist*, no. 78, p. 526.

20. Cohens v. Virginia, 6 Wheaton 264 (1821), 404.

21. Jefferson to George Wythe, June, 1776, in *Writings of Thomas Jefferson*, 1:410. Emphasis added.

22. *Federalist*, no. 48, p. 333.

23. McCulloch v. Maryland, 4 Wheaton 316 (1819).

24. Andrew Jackson, veto message of July 10, 1832, in *Messages and Papers*, ed. Richardson, 2:582.

25. The impeachment power is in Art. I, secs. 2 and 3; the exceptions clause is in Art. III, sec. 2; congressional power over the size of the Court arises from the fact that no number is constitutionally established (see Art. III, sec. 1).

26. *Federalist*, no. 81, p. 546.

27. *Writings of Thomas Jefferson*, 15:213.

28. Art. III, sec. 2.

29. Edward S. Corwin, *The Constitution and What it Means Today*, rev. Harold W. Chase and Craig Ducat, 13th ed. (Princeton: Princeton University Press, 1973), p. 178.

30. 7 Wallace 506 (1869), 514.

31. Turner v. Bank of North America, 4 Dallas 8 (1799), 10n1. See also Carey v. Curtis, 3 Howard 236 (1845), 245; Sheldon v. Sills, 8 Howard 441 (1850), 449; Daniels v. Railroad, 3 Wallace 250 (1865), 254; The *Francis Wright*, 105 U.S. 381 (1881), 386; Lockerty v. Phillips, 319 U.S. 182 (1943), 187.

32. Leonard G. Ratner, "Congressional Power over the Appellate Jurisdiction of the Supreme Court," *University of Pennsylvania Law Review* 109 (December 1960):157–202.

33. Scigliano, *Supreme Court and the Presidency*, pp. 10–11.

34. Henry M. Hart, Jr., "The Power of Congress to Limit the Jurisdiction of Federal Courts," *Harvard Law Review* 66 (June 1953):1362–1402. See also Lawrence Gene Sager, "Constitutional Limitations on Congress' Authority to Regulate the Jurisdiction of the Federal Courts," *Harvard Law Review* (November 1981):17–89. *Villanova Law Review* 22 (May 1982):893–1041 contains major articles on both sides of this issue.

35. United States v. United Mine Workers of America, 330 U.S. 258 (1947), 308 (concurring opinion).

36. The first child labor law (39. Stat. 675) was passed in 1916 and voided by the Court in Hammer v. Dagenhart, 247 U.S. 251 (1918). The second child labor law, the Child Labor Tax Act (40 Stat. 1138), was passed in 1919 and voided in 1922 in Bailey v. Drexel Furniture Co., 259 U.S. 20. The third such law, in 1938 (52 Stat. 1060, secs. 3 and 12), was upheld in United States v. Darby, 312 U.S. 100 (1941).

37. McCullom v. Board of Education, 333 U.S. (1948), and Zorach v. Clausen, 343 U.S. 306 (1952).

38. Berger, *Congress v. the Supreme Court*, p. 195.

39. See United States v. Cruikshank, 92 U.S. 542 (1875), and United States v. Harris, 106 U.S. 629 (1882).

40. See the Civil Rights Act of 1964 (28 U.S.C., secs. 201 and 202). The act was upheld in Heart of Atlanta Motel v. United States, 379 U.S. 241 (1964), and Katzenbach v. McClung, 379 U.S. 294 (1964).

41. Quoted in Gerald Gunther and Noel T. Dowling, *Constitutional Law*, 8th ed. (Mineola, N.Y.: Foundation Press, 1970), p. 33.

42. See, for example, Jones v. Alfred H. Mayer Co., 392 U.S. 409 (1968).

43. 297 U.S. 1 (1936). The second AAA was upheld in Mulford v. Smith, 307 U.S. 38 (1939). The quotation is from Henry Abraham, *The Judicial Process* (New York: Oxford University Press, 1968), p. 334.

44. Corwin, *Court over Constitution*, p. 74. See also p. 61.

45. Lincoln, speech at Chicago, July 10, 1858, in *Collected Works*, 2:495.

46. Act of June 19, 1862, 12 U.S. Statutes at Large 432. For the constitutional arguments in Congress over the passage of the bill, see *Congressional Globe*, 37th Cong., 2d sess. (1862), pt. 3, pp. 2041–54, 2066–68.

47. Lincoln, speech at Springfield, June 26, 1857, in *Collected Works*, 2:401.

48. Jackson, veto message of July 10, 1832, in *Messages and Papers*, ed. Richardson, 2:582.

49. Lincoln, speech at Springfield, July 17, 1858, in *Collected Works*, 2:516.

50. Roe v. Wade, 410 U.S. 113 (1973), and Doe v. Bolton, 410 U.S. 179 (1973).

51. See Stephen L. Wasby, *The Supreme Court in the Federal Judicial System* (New York: Holt, Rinehart & Winston, 1978), pp. 190–91. On federal funding for abortions, see Harris v. McRae, 448 U.S. 297, and Maher v. Roe, 432 U.S. 464.

52. See p. 127.

53. For a good review of the various bills that Congress has considered in order to place formal restrictions on the exercise of judicial review (e.g., requiring an extraordinary majority on the Court to void a federal law), see Walter F. Murphy, *Congress and the Court* (Chicago: University of Chicago Press, 1962), pp. 3–34, 63.

54. United States v. Guest, 383 U.S. 745 (1966), 783n7 (concurring and dissenting opinions).

55. Oregon v. Mitchell, 400 U.S. 112 (1970), 143. See also Ex parte Virginia, 100 U.S. 339 (1879), 345–46.

56. Katzenbach v. Morgan, 384 U.S. 641 (1966), 668 (Harlan dissenting).

57. The leading statement of this position is Gary McDowell, "A Modest Remedy for Judicial Activism," *Public Interest*, Spring 1982, pp. 3–20.

58. Ibid., p. 6.

59. *Writings of James Madison*, 5:294.

60. Marshall to Chase, January 23, 1804, in Albert J. Beveridge, *The Life of John Marshall*, 4 vols. (Boston: Houghton Mifflin, 1916–19), 3:177.

6   The Promise and Perils of an Active Court

Epigraph: Bickel, *Least Dangerous Branch*, p. 25.

1. *Federalist*, no. 10, p. 61; no. 71, p. 482. See also Martin Diamond, "Democracy and *The Federalist*: A Reconsideration of the Framers' Intent," *American Political Science Review* 53 (March 1959):52–68.

2. *Federalist*, no. 47, p. 324.

3. Ibid., no. 78, pp. 526, 522.

4. Ibid., no. 48, p. 332.

5. Ibid., no. 9, p. 51.

6. Myers v. United States, 272 U.S. 52 (1926), 293 (Brandeis dissenting).

7. Charles C. Pinckney, speech of August 27, 1787, in *Records of the Federal Convention*, ed. Farrand, 2:429.

8. George Mason, speech of June 21, 1787, in ibid., p. 78.

9. Cardozo, *Nature of the Judicial Process*, p. 94.

10. Bickel, *Least Dangerous Branch*, p. 82.

11. Madison, speech of June 4, 1787, in *Records of the Federal Convention*, ed. Farrand, 1:110.

12. Henry M. Hart, Jr., "Foreward: The Time Chart of the Justices," *Harvard Law Review* 73 (1959):99.

13. Bailyn, *Ideological Origins*, p. 161.

14. *Works of John Adams*, 4:113.

15. Lincoln, speech at Springfield, June 26, 1857, in *Collected Works*, 2:406.

16. Bickel, *Least Dangerous Branch*, p. 25.

17. See John Agresto, "The Limits of Judicial Supremacy: The Case for Checked Activism," *Georgia Law Review* 14 (Spring 1980):471–95.

18. *Federalist*, no. 51, pp. 352–53. See also chap. 1 above, pp. 26–27 and 30–31.

19. *Federalist*, no. 10, p. 64.

20. See further Cox, *Role of the Supreme Court*, p. 115.

21. Works damning the legislative process and elevating the virtues of judicial government are legion. Recent examples are Abram Chayes, "The Role of Judges in Public Law Litigation," *Harvard Law Review* 89 (1976):1281, and Richard Neely, *How Courts Govern America* (New Haven: Yale University Press, 1983). This observation is also directed at the Ely and Choper books discussed in the Preface.

22. See pp. 11–12 and 34–36, above.

23. See Wright, "Role of the Supreme Court," p. 26.

24. A. F. of L. v. American Sash Door Co., 335 U.S. 538 (1949), 556 (Frankfurter concurring).

25. Corwin, *Twilight of the Supreme Court*, p. 122.

26. See Cox, "New Dimensions," pp. 813–20.

27. Horowitz, *Courts and Social Policy*, p. 6.

28. *Writings of Thomas Jefferson*, 15:213.

29. *Federalist*, no. 47.

30. Ibid., no. 78, pp. 522–23.

31. Thayer, "Origin and Scope," pp. 155–56.

32. Rostow, "Democratic Character," p. 213. See Black, *People and the Court*, p. 89.

33. Cardozo, *Nature of the Judicial Process*, p. 94.

34. Lincoln, *Collected Works*, 4:271.

35. Bickel, *Least Dangerous Branch*, pp. 240, 244. See also Alexander Bickel, *The Supreme Court and the Idea of Progress* (New York: Harper & Row, 1970), p. 91.

Index

Library of Congress Cataloging in Publication Data
AGRESTO JOHN
   The Supreme Court and constitutional democracy.

   Includes bibliographical references and index.
      1. Judicial power—United States.   2. United States.
Supreme Court.   3. Judicial review—United States.
4. Separation of powers—United States.   I. Title.
KF5130.A93   1984   347.73'262   83-45928
ISBN 0-8014-1623-X   (alk. paper)   347.307352